OF CHAFF AND WHEAT

Of Chaff and Wheat

Writers, War, and Treason

Jean Paulhan

Translated from the French and
with an Introduction by Richard Rand

University of Illinois Press
Urbana and Chicago

Manufactured in the United States of America
C 5 4 3 2 1

∞ This book is printed on acid-free paper.

Library of Congress Cataloging-in-Publication Data
Paulhan, Jean, 1884–1968.
[De la paille et du grain, English]
Of chaff and wheat : writers, war, and treason /
Jean Paulhan ; translated from the French and with
an introduction by Richard A. Rand.
p. cm.
ISBN 0-252-02924-0 (cloth : alk. paper)
I. Rand, Richard A. (Richard Aldrich) II. Title.
PQ2631.A85D413 2004
840.9'00912—dc22 2003022911

CONTENTS

ACKNOWLEDGMENTS

My heartfelt thanks to all those assisting in this enterprise, among them the anonymous readers of the manuscript, Stephen Barnett, Yve-Alain Bois, Roger Chartier, John Crowley, Janine and Guillaume des Forêts, Danielle Mémoire, the late Louis-René des Forêts, Christian Garaud, Robert Olin, Jacqueline Paulhan, Jean-Kely Paulhan, Sebastian Rand, Willis G. Regier, Anne Simonin, Michael Syrotinski, Harold Weber, Patrick Weil, Toby Whitman, Sylvio Yeschua, and Messody Zrihen.

TRANSLATOR'S INTRODUCTION

Jean Paulhan (1884–1968) wrote *De la paille et du grain* [*Of Chaff and Wheat*] as a protest against the Comité Nationale des Ecrivains—the "National Committee of Writers," or Céné (the literary arm of the French Resistance)—after it had blacklisted writers accused of collaborating with the Germans during World War II. Paulhan, who had helped to found the Céné in 1941, spoke out against the blacklisting at the first public meeting of the committee in the fall of 1944, then tendered his resignation in 1946 and published this book in 1948.

As a work of its particular moment, speaking to that moment in exact detail, *Of Chaff and Wheat* may seem at times to bury itself in the grave of its own ephemera; but it also summons the reader to that gravesite as a statement of the political convictions that Paulhan had developed during the previous half-century. Treating topics like community, nation, homeland, party, partisanship, loyalty, patriotism, and democracy as issues of language and literature, *Of Chaff and Wheat* builds, in particular, upon the reflections elaborated in *Les fleurs de Tarbes* [The flowers of Tarbes, 1941], Paulhan's major treatise on rhetoric composed throughout the 1920s and 1930s.

Suffering a vaguely articulated reputation for political naiveté or incorrectness, *Of Chaff and Wheat* has long been regarded with a measure of perplexity that contributes to the marginalizing of Paulhan's work overall (*De la paille et du grain* has been out of print in France for over a decade). There are indeed moments when the book, if read a little carelessly, can sound as if written by a nationalist or a cultural imperialist—promoting a unified France, political harmony among the French, and a well-regulated French language as the key to cultural unity. Occasional passages can tempt us to suppose that Paulhan subscribes to such positive pieties: when, for example, he attacks Louis Aragon's claims to patriotism, he can lead the reader to suppose that he lays claim to a more genuine patriotism for himself, something he never does (Paulhan offers frequent precautions against deductive fallacies of this kind).

Of Chaff and Wheat, then, poses a variety of practical demands on today's reader, among them the need to gain a close familiarity with the details of its historical context, and with Paulhan's views as well, on the specifics of literary writing. But the main requirement is a survey of Paulhan's views on language in general.

THE RESISTANT

When he published this book in 1948, Paulhan—already renowned as an editor for Gallimard and the *Nouvelle Revue Française,* as a rhetorician and linguist, and as a writer of fiction, ethnography, art criticism, and literary criticism—was also celebrated for his role as "Director" of the Resistance's publishing operations. His wartime activities, which have yet to be told in precise, encyclopedic detail, include the following episodes:

—In November 1940, five months after the armistice, Paulhan joined one of the early Resistance networks, the circle of the Musée de l'Homme, which had merged with an anarchist group called Les Amis d'Alain-Fournier. During the following March, he attempted to print a broadside entitled *Resistance* on a Roneotype machine in his apartment. Warned of an imminent raid—the Gestapo, in fact, had already penetrated the network—Paulhan took the machine apart and dropped it, piece by piece, into the waters of the Seine (not for Paulhan an entirely painful exercise: as he put it in a letter to his friend Guillaume de Tarde in 1909, "It's fun to demolish machines. In the regiment, they taught me how to disassemble a locomotive . . . I hope to put this to good use someday. Revenge for the one who didn't learn physics . . . nothing nobler, or easier, than demolishing"). In May of that year, however, the Gestapo proceeded to arrest Paulhan and subjected him to intense interrogation and solitary confinement. He was released a week thereafter only through the intervention of his friend and Gallimard colleague, the collaborator Drieu la Rochelle (other members of the network were not so fortunate, five of them being sent to the firing squad on 23 February 1942). Throughout the war Paulhan would continue to work, as he had for the two decades preceding, at the Editions Gallimard, in an office adjoining the one occupied by Drieu himself—Drieu having assumed, with Paulhan's encouragement, the Directorship of the *Nouvelle Revue Française* shortly after the start of the Occupation.

—In the fall of 1941, with his resistance colleague Jacques Decour, Paulhan attempted to publish *La Pensée Libre*, a journal that also collapsed when the Gestapo raided its printing press.

—Again, in the fall of 1941, at the behest of Louis Aragon and the National Front, Paulhan established, with Decour and five others, the Comité Nationale des Ecrivains (Céné). Concurrently, and also with Decour, Paulhan founded a periodical for the Céné entitled the *Lettres Françaises*, which, in its own turn, was suppressed by yet another wave of arrests. Decour was captured by the Gestapo shortly thereafter and sent to the firing squad on 30 May 1942. Notwithstanding this catastrophic interruption, the *Lettres Françaises* began to appear on a regular basis during the fall of that year.

—In 1942, Paulhan assisted in the founding of the review *Messages* and the *Editions de Minuit*, a small publishing house managed by the writer Vercors (Jean Bruller). During the Occupation, in effect, Paulhan would serve as the principle traffic director and fund-raiser for resistance publications throughout the hexagon.

—In May 1944, once again the target of the Gestapo, and advised of this fact by the collaborator Marcel Jouhandeau, Paulhan went into hiding for two months in the house of Georges Bataud, an old acquaintance connected to the Action Française (the right-wing, nationalist organization founded by Charles Maurras).

—In September 1944, when the Céné voted to pursue the blacklisting of collaborators, Paulhan launched a protest that would play out for the better part of the next ten years.

"WE MEN OF THE LEFT"

Although Paulhan calls himself a "man of the Left," *Of Chaff and Wheat* provides very little information about his political history. He was, in fact, recruited as a Resistance leader by the directors of the National Front, the wartime "ghost," as it were, of the Popular Front—the leftist alliance governing France prior to the Occupation. Paulhan had himself participated in the Popular Front, winning, in 1935, a seat on the city council of Châtenay-Malabry for the S.F.I.O. (the Socialist Party), running on a ticket formed by Jean Longuet, the great-grandson of Karl Marx. Paulhan held that seat until 1940, achieving, among other things, the construction of a public-financed swimming pool for the city.

From what political position, then, was Paulhan moved to attack his colleagues on the Left in 1944 and thereafter, even as he continued to salute them as his friends? Paulhan can appear on occasion to be almost lenient towards the collaborationist writers who were being blacklisted. Indeed, he never denounces the authors targeted by the Céné—fascists, supporters of the Vichy regime, some of them convicted as traitors in 1945 (such as Lucien Rebatet and Charles Maurras), some of them sentenced to death, and one (Robert Brasillach) even sent to the firing squad. It is with a surprising degree of vehemence, indeed, that Paulhan denounces his leftist colleagues—especially Louis Aragon, Louis Martin-Chauffier, Jean Cassou, and Julien Benda, who had worked with him during his directorship, from 1925 to 1940, at the *Nouvelle Revue Française.* Was Paulhan shifting, perhaps, to the right? Or was he acting on right-wing convictions previously undisclosed? Or did he lack strong convictions in the first place? Paulhan sometimes expressed, for example, a qualified respect for the monarchist Charles Maurras—and there was, in fact, a political basis for that respect. It could even be said to hold a key to Paulhan's broader political orientation: he was in agreement with Maurras, not as a nationalist, but as an anti-Republican, the common cause for those on the Left and the Right—anarchists as well as monarchists—who were opposed to representative government.

ANARCHISM

Paulhan's conflict within the Céné comprises an episode in his lifelong commitment to anarchism (a commitment, or career, that has yet to be studied with scholarly care). In his student days, shortly after the turn of the century, Paulhan affiliated himself with Jean Grave, the French disciple of the Russian Peter Kropotkin. He was introduced to Grave and his circle in 1904 by a group of young Russian and Polish women—Jewish university students living in exile in his parents' boardinghouse, among them Rosa Gerchgorine (Paulhan's first love); Ida Sviette (jailed, then executed, upon returning to Poland in 1905); and Sala Prusak (whom Paulhan would marry in 1911 and who became the mother of his two sons).

Grave's and Kropotkin's concept of anarchism was of an individualist rather than a syndicalist persuasion—close to Bakunin and Tolstoy and at odds with the politics of Marx and Engels. It was antiparliamentarian, antiauthoritarian, anti-Soviet, anticlerical, and antimonarchical—and also nonviolent in the workplace (opposed, in other words, to the practice of sabotage) and nonpacifist in foreign affairs (Paulhan joined the army in 1904 and was wounded on the front lines at the start of World War I). As an anarchist during the twenties and thirties, Paulhan repeatedly quarreled with the Communists, breaking, in 1927, with his surrealist colleagues Eluard and Aragon after they joined the French Communist Party. And though, with some plausibility, we could read Paulhan's attacks on the Céné in the mid-forties as a replay of those earlier quarrels, such a reading would miss the affirmative tendency of Paulhan's anarchism—its radically democratic orientation. As the editor of the *Nouvelle Revue Française,* for example, it was Paulhan's exceptional practice to publish writers of the Left and Right on any given topic in any given issue—turning the journal into a platform for something he called the "extreme middle"—one opportunity, among others, to pursue his anarchism's democratic tendency.

When Paulhan discusses democracy, he invariably resorts to a figure, or rhetorical character, which he calls *le premier venu,* or "the man of the street." It is at once a *figure* of speech (for the commonality of the common) and a figure of (or about) *speech,* a metaphor for the relationship between humans and language giving rise to their commonality. We can find a particularly forthright elaboration of this figure—which organizes or animates *Of Chaff and Wheat* from the sidelines, enigmatically—in an essay of 1938 entitled "La démocratie appelle au premier venu" [Democracy calls for the man of the street], an essay not in itself obviously concerned with rhetoric and language. I translate it here in extenso:

> If I try to reduce democracy to its essential features, I find the following:
>
> First of all, the individual is worth more than the State: because society is made for man, not man for society; quite a few sociologists believe that nations have a soul. Quite a few unanimists hold that every group is a god; and quite a few political realists, that only the fasces is moral, just, and strong. But democracy was invented in opposition to sociologists, political realists, and even unanimists. Whatever the rationale for our existence—whatever marvelous thing may befall us, and give us the right to live, and sometimes to die—democracy knows at least *where* the rationale can be found, *where* the event happens. In a word, it accepts the person, and the person suffices for it. That's the first point.
>
> It involves *everyone,* red or black—that's the second point. Sick, drunk, or unfaithful. Because democracy opposes racism as much as it opposes totalitarian governments. It claims that a strange quality exists in man, such that no man could ever completely reject it (not even in labor camps). The Declaration of Rights tells us that men are born equal—something easily admitted. It adds that they *stay* so, which is certainly more singular. But this singularity pertains to the doctrine *also.* Democracy has its mystery, like religion; and its secret, like poetry.
>
> The last aspect of that secret is this: man is valued more for what is natural, immediate, and naive about him than for anything he acquires. A great expert has merit: but a mere man is more precious, and even more extraordinary, than a great expert.
>
> When we want to build a bridge, a castle, or a newspaper, we're happy to hire an architect, an engineer, a journalist. But when we build a nation, we must first call on someone who isn't a journalist or an architect. On the man of the street, who could be a ditch dig-

ger, a strawberry merchant, or nothing at all. Democracy calls for *the man of the street* [*le premier venu*] instead of aristocrats—intellectual aristocrats in particular. And we can easily see why: the man of the street keeps in touch with essentials. A linguist can spend his whole life studying the origin of a language (he's wrong). An architect can be obsessed in his dreams by a concert hall where concerts sound good. But the man of the street has only the joys, sorrows, and accidents of everyday life to call his own (especially the kinds of accident mentioned above). He has to be content with them. He has to be consumed with them.

Such is democracy. I don't call it wise or reasonable. I don't want to convince anyone. And besides, it's blindingly clear that we don't live in a democracy [. . .]

[. . .] In a good democracy, decisions would fall to the mason. With us, no—everything's done with princes.

We know how. All the patient work of France's committees and lodges, small groups and cells in the sections and subsections of our major parties—we can sing praises for their work, as they create investitures and candidates, deputies and senators, votes by deputies and senators, laws, and even foreign affairs: we can sing the praises of all these things: the work accomplished is intelligent and tedious, studious and (for the most part) disinterested, subtle and universal. It generates millions of texts and documents. It assembles hundreds of thousands of people. Finally there's nothing else to say, except for one thing: this isn't a democracy. It patiently schools and cultivates an aristocracy of knowledge, thought, and eloquence. And God help me from saying anything against intelligence. We need it. We need experts and technicians. But I believe—at least as a democrat—that when technicians and experts disagree (as they usually do), then the last word should fall—not to an arrangement between specialists who agree among themselves and upset the rest of us—but instead to the Arbitrage, to the Arbitrariness, of someone who isn't witting, astute, talented, or especially gifted with eloquence—or learned, or a sports hero of some kind. Of someone who doesn't owe his standing to his brilliant merits, his charm, or a plebiscite. I repeat, the man of the street. ("La démocratie appelle au premier venu," OC 5:277–82)

When he calls democracy a "doctrine" or "mystery," Paulhan means that it posits, in faith rather than reason, an absolute equality between individuals. Of the three terms in the formula "liberty, equality, fraternity," equality is not merely primus inter pares—it belongs to a more comprehensive order of values than the other two. Oligarchies (and republics) are, from this standpoint, little more than imperfect, unrealized democracies. Paulhan, as indicated above, is particularly interested in the (antidemocratic) tendencies of expertise: for him, an expert is first and foremost a non-expert who forgets where he came from. Paulhan pictures society as an endless conflict among equals inequitably equipped, experts who gain economic and political mastery at all times over the man of the street—over, most importantly, the "man of the street" that the expert himself shall have always, already, been. The king himself, for Paulhan, is first and foremost a man of the street.

Paulhan focuses his proposition more precisely still: where the expert joins "an aristocracy of knowledge, mind, and eloquence," the man of the street is "not witting, astute, talented, or particularly gifted in eloquence," not "learned." Education sets the expert apart: it gives rise to specialized elites by building their expertise on properties actually shared by everyone—in particular, on a common competence in speech, in the speaking of the vernacular. This common competence is recognized, in a democracy, by the shared service of jury duty—by what Paulhan calls the "Arbitrage," or the "Arbitrariness," of judging. For Paulhan, competence in a language—which is not to be confused with literacy—enfranchises individuals; a body politic tending toward democracy bears, as the portents of its shared linguistic franchise, the rights and responsibilities of legal judgment. The principle of linguistic equality itself arises from some surprising premises.

THE MOTHER TONGUE

> Je crois que le langage contient la clef de tous les problèmes qui nous preoccupent. [I think language holds the key to all the problems bothering us.]
>
> —*Entretien avec Robert Mallet*

The "mother tongue"—the locus of social existence for Paulhan, and hence the womb, or matrix, of any possible politics—is not a "natural" natural language. For Paulhan, language is artificial, conventional, and he regards any view to the contrary as a kind of dream. Born into a Francophone family, Paulhan loves to deny that he finds his French mother tongue in any way natural, domestic, or even familiar. Referring to his own linguistic history, he volunteers the following remark: "I know Malagasy, Malay, and Javanese; I read German and Dutch. That's all. But I had several biases: or at least a general bias: I always saw French as a foreign language. I've never stopped learning it. Malagasy, on the other hand, very quickly struck me as a *natural* language. Something strange happened to me: I found I was eloquent in Malagasy. French is completely different" (OC 4:499). Just as Paulhan's mother tongue is foreign—and in that respect not natural to him—so the language of his "natural" eloquence is not maternal, not matricial (Paulhan actually learned Malagasy at the age of twenty-four).

Not only does a person maintain, then, the proximity of a foreigner to the mother tongue; Paulhan considers every person bilingual: each of us speaks an idiolect that is not, in itself, a fully articulated or shared language, but which is nonetheless exterior to us and, however faintly and asymmetrically so, potentially communicable to our fellow man—a meaningful, if feeble, idiolect. Paulhan likes to analyze the operations of this idiolect in his prose fiction, especially in the allegorizing anecdotes that he calls his "causes célèbres." We find one such anecdote in a journal entry dating from 1945, in which Paulhan describes a kiss—rhapsodic, singular, and exemplary—as "a gift of tongues" (and we recall that his last major rhetorical treatise, published in 1967, is entitled *Le don des langues* [The gift of tongues]). Here, he addresses a woman called Diana:

> When we first kissed, Diana, you offered just one lip, slightly swollen, stiff and dry. But the second time, I thought I felt your two lips at once, and your teeth and tongue close together, and felt them quicken brusquely with a movement that I found mysterious—a movement beyond pleasure, agitating, differently at each moment, your teeth and the inside of your lips—an inexplicable movement imparting pleasure all the more thrilling for being unstudied. And then I finally understood that you were talking [*vous parliez*], that I was being given a chance to receive your most intimate speech [*parole*], hardly separated from the mind [*esprit*], when it wasn't even speech [*quand elle n'était pas encore parole*]. And I felt a great emotion.
>
> What were you saying? I think I heard: "I should not . . . I should not . . ." Yes, I think I heard that. I sensed that a sacred event had

> passed between us, that no one had ever given me, no one would ever give me, more than you gave at that moment. (*La vie est pleine des choses redoutables,* 270)

Diana's intimate speech is an isolated and exposed speech, situated, in fact, on the outside of two "insides" at once—on the outside of her mind [*esprit*] and on the outside of her mother tongue. Separated from her mind, this intimate speech has yet to achieve its alteration, or translation, into French. Paulhan himself has to convert it into French—before responding in French—through a speculative act of translation, and the possibility that Diana might have happened upon her "most intimate speech" by way of French in the first place does not alter this topology.

POLITICAL CREATURES

> Je n'ai cessé, de vrai, de trouver dans les arguments le fait primitif, l'instinct de conservation de tout langage. [In truth, I never stopped finding the original fact, the survival instinct of every language, in arguments.]
>
> —*La vie est pleine des choses redoubtables*

> Enfin je suis porté à penser que les relations de l'homme avec son langage sont les plus graves de toutes, ou mieux commandent toutes les autres—et qu'il y a une terrible vérité dans le mot de Dawson que "c'est la rhétorique de Cicéron qui a fait l'Europe." [I finally came to believe that a man's ties to his language are the most serious of all ties, or, better yet, that they govern all others—and that there's a terrible truth to Dawson's dictum that "Cicero's rhetoric created Europe."]
>
> —*Choix de lettres*

All human interactions, for Paulhan, are versions of Diana's kiss—attempts to communicate into, out of, with, and against the mother tongue, and from a place oblique or alien to that tongue. There is no bond between humans unmediated by this priority, this a priori, of translation. And languages always change: they disclose their forms even as they lose them. Frail, finite, and mortal, languages cannot build or maintain conventions on their own, but have to enlist, as it were, human beings to pursue the maintenance of those conventions. When humans accept this challenge, communities start to take shape (*Of Chaff and Wheat* describes this process of bonding as a "festival"). Concurrently, for Paulhan, every individual, as an isolated speaker of his or her own idiolect, exists in a state of weakness such that, to maintain the viability of his or her idiolect, he or she has to labor within the mother tongue, contributing, with more or less force, to its building and unbuilding. Participants in this traffic operate in a state of perpetual conflict with (and within) a language, in a state of mutual contest or collision (social, asocial, or antisocial)—for which the word "community," presupposing as it does an advanced degree of consensus and integration, may not be the most pertinent or timely term. Collaborative interactions are errant and conflictual. Indeed, the basis of democracy—a general will to maintain the common tongue—is a pathway to the very mastery or expertise in language that undermines democracy.

"Rhetoric" is the name Paulhan assigns to this universal and conflictual traffic: all languages and literatures, for him, are irreducibly rhetorical, forensic, argumentative. And rhetoric comprises the history of a language as well; or more precisely, Paulhan assigns the word "history" to the play of rhetoric as the endlessly warring formation of the mother tongue. Therefore the mother tongue also fulfills a specifically historical function in a narrow sense: it serves as an archive of argumentative moves, moves which, for Paulhan, occur at the level of word and phrase—at the level, in particular, of the proverb, the cliché, or the received idea. We know history insofar as we know a language, with its reservoir of (historically constructed) idioms and commonplaces.

As a summary of Paulhan's logic, consider a journal passage dating from the 1920s in which he recalls the moment at which he discovered the rhetorical grounds of language. He recounts it as a story of three "flashes," of three *éclairs,* that came to him in Algiers during the winter and spring of 1912–13. Since the journal passage is very long, I offer it below in paraphrase.

The first *éclair* is an insight into the irreducibly forensic, argumentative nature of language. Paulhan calls this forensic tendency in language *le rayonnement de l'argument qui devient proverbe*—"the radiance of an argument becoming a proverb." He will explore this insight with elaborate care in his lifelong study of proverbs and commonplaces—analyzing their micrological (semantic and grammatical) features as arguments ready-to-hand ("might makes right" or "once bitten, twice shy," for example). We are born among these "proverbial" networks of disputation, of which the literary work is a highly elaborated form.

The second *éclair* is an insight into the legibility of the equivocal: *le sens est un fait composé, analysable*—"meaning is a composed, analyzable fact." From this premise will issue an increasingly subtle deliberation on the complex tropology (and topology) of language as word, thing, and idea in *Les fleurs de Tarbes* and *Le don des langues*. Any speaker who learns to practice the received (proverbial) ideas embedded in his mother tongue argues in that language on the basis of such a practical analysis or understanding.

The third *éclair*—Nietzschean in its concern for illness and health, weakness and strength—is Paulhan's insight that any language, no matter how "private" or "public," finds itself on the defensive: *le langage employé à sa propre défense*—"language employed in its own defense." The mother tongue has to defend itself through the agency of its speakers, because language is "a weak, artificial formation, felt at all times to be threatened (but especially so during discussions, with their differences of opinions). Therefore this formation must have quickly required a system of protection, of defense . . . with which, however, the language is itself so confused that it can no longer be distinguished from that defensive system. Speech therefore strikes us, for the most part, as an undertaking meant to prove that indeed we *can* speak." (*La vie est pleine des choses redoutables*, 198–204)

Speech, then, is the defensive assertion that one can and shall speak by resorting to a ready-made, and acquired, system of altering verbal defenses. It is the medium and motive for all political action—defensive utterances in defense of a system of linguistic defenses. We fight *for* the language in order to fight *in* the language, and vice versa. Of the principal political entities mentioned in *Of Chaff and Wheat*—nation, state, homeland—none exists apart from language as the weak collective of particular, contesting weaknesses. In life, love, and war we learn, through trial and error, to pursue the contests already embedded in a shared tongue—each of us operating, to borrow the title of Paulhan's first published work of fiction, as a *guerrier appliqué,* or diligent warrior, in words, proverbs, and commonplaces. Paulhan's various *récits* all tell the story of this learning process; *Of Chaff and Wheat* tells it as a story of learning the ruses of political opportunism—the tricks employed by his fellow adepts in the martial arts of rhetoric.

"OUR" TONGUE

> Je ne vois pas un de mes petits livres qui ne soit sorti d'une inquiétude de langage. [I don't see a single one of my little books that doesn't come from an uneasiness about language.]
>
> —*Entretien avec Robert Mallet*

Working from his hypotheses on language, Paulhan develops, in the opening chapter of *Of Chaff and Wheat,* the description of a language gaining and losing its distinctness—a process here taken as a measure of the diligence, or the vacillating confidence, of its speakers. The language at issue, French, is spoken and written at a time when the inhabitants of the hexagon suffer, in Paulhan's judgment, from a weakening of linguistic will:

> What a pleasure to read, in the last pages from Eugene Marsan: "this horse has two *joquets . . .*" *Joquet,* like *croquet,* like *jacquet,* makes for a nice French word. Ah, just this week I also saw, I don't remember where, "the train ran on the *relles,*" and "let's play *foute-balle.*" And we go looking for prize-winning authors! Here they are. We'll never lack for idiots (myself among them, but I plan to change) who say *mitinnng*—unpronounceable, really, a kind of ringing—for something they write as "meeting"; and say *hapéfiou* for "happy few"; and even consider themselves distinguished! And see themselves, precisely, as the *hapéfious* (when they could call themselves the *fine-fleur,* like everyone else). Around 1910, the people would boldly say *métingue*—like *meringue,* or *fringues*—and Gourmont would write it down. Since then . . . the semiexperts among us enjoy lots of prestige, and Gourmont never found a successor.

In his argument, Paulhan distinguishes two kinds of words deriving from English: words that are "nice" [*gentil*] in French, such as *joquet* [jockey], *croquet* [croquet], *jacquet* [jacket], *relle* [rail], *foute-balle* [football], and *métingue* [meeting]; and words that are not nice in French, such as "meeting," "happy few," "containers," and "trusteeship." As with any word in French, the nice and the not-nice words come from a foreign language, preserving, in some degree, their original meanings, but differing from each other in their phonetic and orthographic forms. Where nice words look and sound French, not-nice words do neither of these—no assimilation to French has been attempted. Where nice words have been willed into French—against a resistance posed both by the foreign word and the French language—not-nice words, adopted by speakers with a diminished will-to-language, are not subjected to any adoptive process: not-nice words are *merely* foreign, a mark of the speaker's indifference to the mother tongue. Thus, where the "bold" [*brave*] speakers of French in 1910 pronounced and wrote *métingue*—a nice French rendering of the English word "meeting"—speakers in 1948, who are not bold, pronounce (as "mitinnng") and write (as *meeting*) a not-nice rendering of that same English word. Due process has been ignored: only the bold invoke, as it were, an appeal on behalf of an appealing word before the tribunal of the language itself—that tribunal being the archive of idiomatic (phonetic and graphic) French materials; and given the imperfection of any tongue—an incompleteness that provides its speakers with unending occasions for its amendment—this adoptive process, for Paulhan, is itself a sign of health.

Such, we should recall, is the view of an anarchist who attaches no positive value to political institutions—not to the nation-state, not to a federation of nation-states, not to an international league or movement (Garry Davis, the "citizen of the world," was one of Paulhan's personal heroes). When Paulhan discusses something called "France," he rarely does so in terms of ethnicity, religion, race, class, gender, or of national or imperial interests (his apparent indifference, throughout the 1950s, to the Algerian independence movement has to be read in this context). For Paulhan, the language called "French" has an almost arbitrary, contingent relationship to anything designated by the adjective "French" or by the noun "France." Not even French "French," as opposed, say, to Canadian "French," belongs to the French or to France. To be sure, the various lives of French, of French speakers, and of France are complexly interinvolved: all are finite and mortal, differing only in the probable length of their life spans. French preceded France and may survive it: Paulhan, near the end of the book, even imagines the possible disappearance of France, surrendering its sovereignty to another nation—as a means of abolishing nationalism: "It may well be the case," he says, that "if our nationalisms are to be abolished, Europe will require the preliminary triumph of *one* nationalism to accomplish that goal." Conversely, the French may seek to preserve France by abandoning French. And while Paulhan regrets and resists this possibility, he never finds it unthinkable. Rather, he poses it as an issue of public health—he deplores the symptoms of a weakened relationship (or loveless marriage) between the language and its speakers. The stronger the language, the stronger the contest between its speakers, and the stronger the speech of the individual.

BLACKLISTING

> J'ai grand respect pour les juges et les hommes de la police. Je suppose qu'ils sont nécessaires, il m'arrive de les admirer (je ne suis pas de ces anarchistes qui veulent que l'écrivain ne relève d'aucune loi). Mais enfin je n'en suis pas un. [I have great respect for judges and policemen. I suppose they're necessary, I've come to admire them (I don't belong to those anarchists who would want writers exempted from every law). But finally I'm not one of them.]
>
> —*De la paille et du grain*

Blacklisting is not a juridical process, and not a legal sanction; it belongs to the political forum, and Paulhan therefore attacks it on rhetorical grounds: blacklisters are weak, and they weaken the readers and writers of the French language, not only by stopping the circulation of works by strong writers—Henri de Montherlant, Jean Giono, and Céline are among those mentioned by Paulhan—but also by resorting to weak arguments in support of their acts of censorship. Paulhan calls such weak arguments "tricks" and "lies": they take the form of misdefining words like "patriot" and "traitor," and of mischaracterizing the blacklisted writers with the words thus misdefined—precluding thereby the clarity, or "exactness," which, for Paulhan, is the most reliable sign of rhetorical strength.

Paulhan tests the boundary between rhetoric and law in his deliberations on the word "treason": he first construes the word as a legal term used, in the courts of law, to describe business done with the enemy—commerce transacted with anyone warring against the state. But then he glosses this definition with a rhetorical twist of his own: a citizen can become, as it were, a rhetorical traitor without incurring legal sanctions. One can betray, as many blacklisted writers did, the country's "cause" without thereby doing business with the enemy. Paulhan cites, as an earlier instance of betraying the cause, the writings of the Céné's most venerable member, Romain Rolland, who, as a French citizen, attacked, in his book *Au-dessus de la mêlée* (1915; *Above the Battle*, 1915), the efforts of France against the Germans in World War I. Paulhan then proceeds to accuse Julien Benda, Louis Aragon, and Paul Eluard—leaders all of the Céné—of having themselves "betrayed the cause of France" with their communist (and pro-Soviet) polemics during the *entre-deux-guerres.* The difference between legal and rhetorical treason enables Paulhan to discriminate between kinds of collaborators and to differentiate between the moments of a given collaborator's career. Thus the fascist Alphonse de Châteaubriant, when writing pro-German material after 1936, merely "betrays the cause of France," but when publishing his weekly journal *La Gerbe* with German funding (from 1940 onward), he "betrays France itself" (for which he was sentenced to death in 1948).

But it is not Paulhan's chief undertaking to praise or blame writers "betraying the cause of France": rather, he seeks to isolate a motive common to those who engage in blacklisting on any side. The motive shared is the commitment to partisan causes within the political forum—notably, but not exclusively, the fascist or the communist causes, which, as international movements, both militate against the independence of France. Just as the French fascists welcomed the German invasion of France, so the French communists were prepared to join forces with the Soviet Union. In this respect, according to Paulhan, neither fascists nor communists can be called patriotic, merely partisan.

The Céné, to be sure, justifies blacklisting as a patriotic exercise, and Paulhan therefore takes that opportunity to develop an analysis of the term "patriotism." To sharpen his analysis, he turns his attention to the concept itself of "the homeland" [*la patrie*] as a piece of language (a word) denoting a rhetorical gesture (a figure of speech). And he makes some fine distinctions. In the first place, he differentiates the "homeland" from the "nation": a "nation," as he puts it, is "the homeland in a raw state, long before any awareness of it, or any wish to belong to it, improve it or defend it." The nation is defined as the basis of an attitude, a collective attitude—"statism" or "nationalism" being names for that attitude. By analogy, patriotism is an attitude as well. Patriotism, for Paulhan, is nationalism intensified to a state of passion, of love—a love for the homeland. Paulhan then essays a definition of the homeland as the object of this passionate attitude:

> But what, then, is patriotism? . . . Well, France is an impetus [*élan*], extending from the Revolution of '89 (and from long before '89) to the revolt of the Maquis. It's also a land of hills and plains tracing their little path from the Rhine to the Pyrenees. And patriotism consists in no longer separating this bodily France from the spiritual France, any more than a man's face is separated from his profile. It's a love for the homeland; it's also the firm will [*la ferme volonté*] to make it better. It's still more: it's deciding to refuse benefits coming from places other than France (just as a child learns to refuse gifts from a stranger). And I won't deny this involves a strange, even a paradoxical feeling. But love has its mysteries.

Paulhan, then, argues a discreet but unequivocal point: the homeland, with its mysteries, is a *figment* of passion. Patriotism, a passionate, mystified attitude, confuses (or fuses) two distinct objects. *On the one hand,* the word "France" can serve as the name for an impetus, an *élan*—the passion of a language-bearing people to persist over long periods of time. Taking its characteristic moments—'89 and the Maquis—as parts for a whole, we might describe this impetus as a conflictual history comprising words and wars—words in French, and acts of war performed by people speaking those words (what Paulhan calls the "spiritual France"). *On the other hand,* however, the word "France" is the name for a terrain, "a land of hills and plains tracing their little path from the Rhine to the Pyrenees"—what Paulhan here calls "the bodily France." But a passion and a terrain are not the same thing, even (or especially) when sharing a common name (the homonym "France"). When the two are confused, then something called *the* "homeland" emerges—not only a possible, but an inevitable, mystification. A mystification of the poetic kind; a little further on, Paulhan returns to this issue:

> In sum, it all happened as if it were dangerous to talk too much about the homeland, unwise to look at it face to face. There exists, then, a mystery of the homeland, as with the mysteries of language, and Letters. Who knows, a neighboring mystery, no doubt. Because confusing the bodily homeland with the spiritual homeland, in order to recognize only *one* homeland, may not be very different, finally, from confusing words with ideas. It's the very same absurdity.

All patriots, finally, commit fundamental errors of this kind. They would include the collaborators as well as their persecutors on the Céné, whose claims to patriotism, however sincere—and Paulhan is willing, now and then, to entertain the possibility that some of the parties are sincere—are neither authoritative nor comprehensive, being partial, partisan, and in error, and therefore (in the spirit of the forum) defensible according to what Paulhan calls "a right to error." Confusing words with ideas remains an absurdity all the same: for words are not essences, but articulations. If indeed "French" exists, and if a forum called "France" exists, they do so, not as essences, but as formations distinct from other languages and forums—as arguments. To argue French well, one really must study it apart, and in acts of rhetorical will. Acts, he says, of "good will": "I can see only too well how hard it is to ponder that homeland; and how, if we ever hope to find it, we'll have to cut through more than one lie or confusion; and how everything about it is waiting for us all—I say: for the best of us—to remake, to re-invent. This is a task worth sharing, at least between men of good will."

MODE D'EMPLOI

The composition of this book is perplexing. Paulhan draws throughout on articles published between 1946 and 1948 (in *Les Temps Modernes, Les Lettres Françaises, Les Nouvelles Épitres, Carrefour, Combat, Le Figaro Littéraire, Gavroche, Les Cahiers du Sud, Les Cahiers de la Pléiade,* and *La Table Ronde*), but he takes care not to assemble them chronologically or to cite the dates and places of their initial publication. Rather, he plays them like cards in a game of bridge (one of his privileged figures for rhetorical practice). *Of Chaff and Wheat* is a *récit,* recounting the Céné's blacklisting activities, Paulhan's responses, and the quarrels arising as a consequence. But it does not tell this story in a simple, straightforward manner: rather, it enacts and repeats the conflict it describes. The first two parts of the book—"An Open Secret," and "From Bridge Enthusiasts to Volunteer Police"—consist of short chapters composed in a familiar, if precious, style, exploring such apparently random topics as the state of the French language, the stupidity of semiexperts, the good sense of the average man, family reunions, Esperanto, bridge, and the coincidence (and inevitable confusion) of word, thing, and idea—of the word *as* word, thing, and idea. Paulhan begins as a writer without axes to grind, without a consuming political passion. Indeed, he defers the discussion of blacklisting until the closing pages of Part II—at which moment, in the space of a single brief chapter ("Of a supplementary police force"), he shifts from describing the Céné's actions in the third person, to addressing the Céné itself in direct apostrophe, his reflective tone turning urgent and hortatory.

In the last sentence of Part II, we meet with a sudden surprise: there we learn that, while Paulhan's apostrophe to the Céné is rightly read as an elevated moment in its chapter—cast in the essay's conventional present tense—it cannot be happening in the present alone. That closing sentence reads: "Here I was violently interrupted." It not only reports, and affects, a rupture (an anacoluthon) in midapostrophe (in midessay); it also indicates—by occurring in the preterite ("Here I *was* violently interrupted")—that the apostrophe thus "interrupted" must itself have occurred at some point in the past, during some discourse by Paulhan (for an unspecified period of time) within an earlier context or forum. Prior to this sentence, we cannot have known that such a forum was in the works (we soon learn that the interruption is, or was, a collective explosion of the Céné).

Thus the violent caesura interrupts two contexts at once—the "here" of the book we read and the "here" of a forum preceding. Or, it splits our reading into heterotopical contexts that cannot, with confidence, be interwoven. The interruption is no mere peripety, or twist, in the plot of a *récit:* the narrative spacing of that *récit* supervenes, as it were, upon the expository spacing of the book's opening essays. It cuts the reader in two: the essay-reader becomes, interruptedly, an indirect witness of the interrupted forum. And the indirect witness promptly becomes its direct witness—because Part III, which immediately follows the interruption, is neither a sequence of essays nor a *récit* but a sheaf of letters—bearing, precisely, the title of "seven letters to the white writers" (as Paulhan calls the blacklisters)—in response to their "violent interruption." The reader, who began the book as Paulhan's sole addressee, ends up reading Paulhan's open mail to other parties, as a random, if interested, witness to their argument. And that argument, in all its contextual complexity, never stops: at the close of the book, Paulhan provides an "appendix" comprising "three notes," his answers to the Céné's (published) responses to the "seven letters." We find ourselves tracking the Céné's replies as they surface in Paulhan's citations, with the exchanges continuing past the end of the volume—beyond it: a few months after *Of Chaff and Wheat,* Paulhan published a "suite" of exchanges in *Les Cahiers de la Pléiade;* and in 1952 he published, as a further installment, his celebrated *Lettre aux directeurs de la resistance* [Letter to the directors of the Resistance], along with attendant replies.

Of Chaff and Wheat is a complex work of intricate composition: through the mechanism of the *récit,* it combines, even as it separates, two discourses addressing two readers. The reader is, and is not, immersed in both discourses. We are admitted, if only as spectators, within the Céné's debate—summoned from outside, as it were, to judge the proceedings inside. But we are summoned after the fact, to witness the argument from a single point of view: for the book is not a record of the proceedings, but a diatribe within those proceedings, a moment within that dispute, presented from the standpoint of one party. And the surrounding dispute, conversely, is itself a moment inscribed within the book's overall argument, so that the book may be said to comprehend the context of which it is a part. More precisely, the book cites those proceedings as an extended example, a kind of cautionary tale, by means of which Paulhan can illustrate his reflections on rhetoric, propounded partly in his opening chapters. As referees, we may hope to judge the debate with detached neutrality; but as readers of Paulhan's book, we are prepared, from the outset, to pass judgment on the Céné and its judgmental blacklisters. Paulhan turns us into a jury, "charging" us to make certain findings, and we are thereby engaged.

Works Cited

Paulhan, Jean. *Choix de lettres.* Vol. 2. Paris: Editions Gallimard, 1992.

———. *Oeuvres Complètes.* 5 vols. Paris: Cercle du Livre Précieux, 1967. Cited herein as OC.

———. *De la paille et du grain.* Paris: Editions Gallimard, 1948.

———. *La vie est plein des choses redoutables.* Paris: Editions Claire Paulhan, 1997.

This translation is dedicated to Jacques Derrida,

bearer of free and patient thoughts.

OF CHAFF AND WHEAT

I

An Open Secret; or, Literature as a Public Festival

JOQUET, *FOUTE-BALLE,* AND *MÉTINGUE*

What a pleasure to read, in the final pages from Eugene Marsan: "this horse has two *joquets . . .*" *Joquet,* like *croquet,* like *jacquet,* makes for a nice French word. Ah, this week I also saw, I don't remember where, "the train ran on the *relles,*" and "let's play *foute-balle.*" And we go looking for prize-winning authors! Here they are. We'll never lack for idiots (myself among them, but I plan to change) who say *mitinnng*—unpronounceable really, a kind of ringing—for something they write as "meeting"; and say *hapéfiou* for "happy few"; and even consider themselves distinguished! And see themselves, precisely, as the *hapéfious* (when they could call themselves the *fine-fleur,* like everyone else). Around 1910, the public would boldly say *métingue*—like *meringue,* or *fringues*—and Gourmont would write it down. Since then . . . the semiexperts among us enjoy lots of prestige, and Gourmont never found a successor. And then there were wars. The chief effect of a war is that everyone generally ends up more convinced than ever: the revolutionary, more revolutionary; the believer, more believing; the impious, much more impious; even the pacifist, who only thinks

Don't say: *hapéfiou.* Say: *la fine fleur.*

that events proved he was right. So everyone ends up more simplistic, more intolerant, and, for that very reason, far more likely to cheat (since things in themselves remain complicated). Language, meanwhile, becomes more obscure. No typical Frenchman today would fail to mention *tankers* and *containers,* or *trusteeship* and *jamboree.* (*Jamboree!*)

According to all the evidence, the contrary should occur: language needs to be simple, and opinions a little complicated.

OF LANGUAGE CONSIDERED AS A BALL

We tend nowadays to see languages (and homelands) as kinds of prisons, as places to flee as we may. Such is the effect of modern philosophy, which is rather somber. And I have no problem with modern philosophy; but I know for a fact that language, with all its baroque or surprising words, actually used to be seen (and still is, by people truly uncultivated), not as a trial at all: as a great public rejoicing. It gives pleasure; it's like a festival, gladly arbitrary and surprising. It can be sung and danced. It even draws crowds (for what's the point of a language, finally, if it doesn't become popular?). It's never happier than when it can crack a good joke about established laws. Sometimes it looks like those mysterious little huts—azur, loafer, bladder, turtle, spatula, ornithorinx—where fights break out between crabs and horned snails. André Gide is amazed that we currently say *pournepaque* (and even, in conversation, *pourpaque*): "I've sent him to the fair, so not to be bored [*pour pas qu'il s'ennuie*]." But the reason is very simple: we say it because it amuses; because it makes for a funny word, like *tarasque* or *fantasque*—a kind of masked ball.

A language is a masked ball.

As with any ball (where we can't show up in caps or suspenders), this one has its rules. Now the main rule is to dress up a foreign word before letting it into the ballroom. Sometimes this turns into a great farce: in *choucroute,* "chou" (almost) means *croute,* and "croute" means *chou.* Mostly we settle for adding false noses: *con-*

tredanse, sabretache, digue, dune, gamin. (Popular words like these—you could call them a folksong.) In the first place, we've always done it this way, and then it's a clear sign, too, of happiness and good health; a sign, as well, of strength. But then we also have to admit that we hardly do this any more. Did we turn bilingual, or trilingual, or plurilingual (clearly seen in the very word to involve something quite hateful)? The question is whether French can still defend itself and disguise in its own way the exotic words it receives. Let the experts do their research here! What will they find? First, that four years of Occupation have left us very few Germanic words (except, obviously, "Nazi," though the flavor of the word is no longer German; and except, too, for *autarchie,*[1] a word that seems even less German than Nazi). Of course there's "Gestapo" (which quickly, and happily, turned into *geste-à-pot*), "Oflag," "Stalag," but these aren't words so much as events, history. And in this respect the Occupation was said to convey, from the very start, the feeling of an historic event. (A very curious feeling it is.) Fine. Perhaps they'll also note that certain English words have disappeared. For instance, do you remember what a *tout* is (pronounced "ta-aout")? Well, according to *Larousse de Poche,*[2] it's "an individual who spies on racehorses, and tries to acquire information about them unknown to others." A funny kind of work. And what can a horse conceal from other horses? It can't even talk. Gone, too, are *railway* and *turf:* we readily say *chemin de fer* and *champ* (for the racecourse). But if you happen to hear "I put my wife on the *turfe* . . . I sent my wife out on the *turfe* . . ."—in the French sense of "street-corner," "sidewalk"—then it's a meaning not to be proud of.

An historic event.

They'll also say, sadly (I hope—but with experts you have to be ready for anything), that we run the risk every day of meeting excellent people called Szrekely, Przyluski, Czackes, Lvov, and even Srb.[3] Now I'd prefer not to cause problems, but it's a fact that we

---

1. *Autarkie* (Greek *autarkeia*).
2. Where I just found it while looking to see whether *tout à fait* needs hyphens. It doesn't.
3. Srb is obviously M. Serbe: and Lvov, Leveau. Przyluski is more puzzling. Why not Chilousque? Or Chilouxe. I don't detest Chilouxe. M. Avtzin signs his novels Claude Aveline. What a good example for everyone. And how we wish Claude Aveline's novels were even better!

can't really like someone if we can't pronounce his name, and if excellent books by M. Przyluski don't enjoy the success they deserve, it's because we're afraid of sounding silly when requesting them at the bookstore. There was a time (and it's up to us to remember this) when Richetti turned into Riquet, and Buckingham into Bouquinquant—the most natural thing on earth, and we never gave it a thought: good, too, for reconciling idiots—afraid (they'd say) of greeting foreigners—with fools who might think of themselves as chauvinists if they happened to francify a foreign name.

What do we want?

Yes, the experts will say all this, and lots of other things too. Which finally comes down to what? To knowing what we want, and whether we have the *desire* to keep speaking French. Fine, let's make up our minds right away and save everyone some time. I'm planning to pulp any book that would run the risk of raising any doubts on the subject.

IT'S NOT A CRIME TO KNOW SEVERAL LANGUAGES

Not without crowning it with flowers, should the opportunity arise. And opportunities do arise. I know of no other book, for example, where Charles du Bos exhibits the virtues and surprises—and, from a certain perspective, the greatness (I have in mind that light and sustained exaltation at which he excels)—of his recently published *Journal.* But still, it's disappointing to watch him escape into English whenever he tries to say something really simple—or, to the contrary, something really subtle (only the in-between is in French).

A misfortune, rather.

Knowing several languages certainly isn't a crime, it's more a misfortune. Perhaps it's due to the poverty of our time; to the poverty, perhaps, of mankind too, and of bourgeois man in particular (since proletarians, or peasants, are perfectly happy with one language). In any case, it's a misfortune that would be stupid to brag about. It's not by being able to say "snail" in three languages that we have a better understanding of the snail; in general, it's quite the contrary (as we see, for example, with du Bos, who never met any).

It's not by being able to discuss intellectualism in seven languages (like members of an international institute) that we become more intelligent. It's quite the contrary. It's not by being able to keep quiet in eighteen languages that we become more eloquent. And I know very well that more than one person believes, deep down, that words, in some mysterious way, reveal the nature of things: unfortunately, this conviction runs the risk of vanishing rather quickly—precisely when we learn a language other than our own.

WELCOME YOUR WORDS AS IDEAS

It's very correct, as they say, that there's a mystery to literature. It's the same as for poetry, and language in general. And it's a very particular mystery, being not in the least bit mysterious or hidden. Perfectly obvious (if we don't watch it too closely). We've all heard of it, we believe in it, and famous writers (and others) have shouted it out from the rooftops. It comes down to one thing: words are *also* ideas. It comes down, if you prefer, to one piece of advice: "Welcome your words as thoughts." (To which I'd gladly add: Treat foreign words as if they didn't mean anything.) And I don't claim that this maxim is clear. No. Considered closely, it's even absurd. It remains to be seen whether, to gain an accurate view of things—particularly of literature—we shouldn't start by putting up with a little absurdity, making it welcome, giving it room.

An open mystery.

In fact, those of our writers who happen to be polyglot have carefully avoided any confusion of vocabularies—fearing a consequent confusion of ideas. Valery Larbaud composes short trilingual poems just as a joke, which he shows only to his friends. And Bernard Groethuysen pushes this scruple to the point of entirely rewriting, in English, an *Anthropology* that he published earlier in German.[4] It's a shame that Charles du Bos didn't follow their ex-

4. It's true that T. S. Eliot uses (and maybe abuses) citations from foreign languages in his early poems. Yes. But only *insofar as this involves* a foreign language,

ample. If only from simple prudence:[5] for where, finally, does the extreme, the abnormal insignificance of, say, *What is Literature?* come from, if not from the following fact: that du Bos reached to the point where he no longer knew for sure what can be said and make sense?

Yes, it's a shame. But it's truly scandalous that an edition published by a French editor for French readers doesn't contain translations of some of the *Journal*'s most serious passages.

The other book is *Stripped Naked,* by Armand Petitjean. In passing, let's crown it with flowers too: it's an honest and ardent essay (or rather a series of little essays) driven by an intense will to coherence. (For me anyway, unless I'm mistaken, it seems to be solving problems, and not just sorting them out.)

WORLD-WIDE THREE

Well, Petitjean has given up most of his prewar mannerisms. He no longer says: "My generation demands . . ." He says amiably, like everyone else: "I want . . ." He no longer cites Klages, Huxley, Jung, or Keyserling at the end of every paragraph: he only cites them once a chapter. But he still has a mania for using every kind of bizarre language. He obstinately says [in English]: "World War Two," or "World War Three" (triage is his thing), when it would be so easy—if *deuxième guerre mondiale* [Second World War] seemed too long—simply to say *la Mondiale-deux* [World-wide two], or *la Mondiale-trois* [World-wide three], just as we still say *l'Empire-deux* [Empire-two], which sounds cleaner and crisper than *le Second Empire* [the Second Empire]. Elsewhere he finds it seriously wrong to say [in English] "ladies love brutes,"[6] because . . . But this has nothing to do with me. I swear I've never talked that way about a woman. Not even in my moments of rage.

---

and because Eliot wants to emphasize the composite, in effect the *false,* character of language available to poets today.

5. Charles du Bos very honestly takes note of the danger. Cf. *Journal,* p. 278.

6. *Les dames aiment les brutes.*

He also provides, as a title to some reflections on Kierkegaard: *Det Einkelte*. Why not *The Solitary*? Or, if he prefers—it's all the same—*The Wild Boar*? Not that I have anything against Danish: there aren't many languages I'd rather learn (Petitjean too, I hope). But finally we treat Danish a little badly if we grant it just one word in a book three hundred pages long. None at all would be better, fairer to both. And let's be frank. When this *Einkelte* wanders into a French text, it's no longer just a solitary. It's a solitary with a tricky nuance (which Petitjean keeps to himself)—as if being a solitary were so important! The solitary has a point, not fully explained. In short, there's a trick of some kind going on. And I don't know if we're often caught using words for reasons and chaff for wheat (as the political journals put it), but something of the sort is happening here.

Be fair to Danish.

Why are we bothered when we read in a novel, for example: "Albert gave Gide's complete works to Madeleine"? Ah! Because we have no idea of what Albert (or the author) intends. Does he want to impress Madeleine? Does he want to pervert her? Does he want to make her more moral? (We never really know what to make of Gide, finally.) Petitjean's *Einkelte* creates problems, confusions, of this kind. It's like the masked ball mentioned above. If we notice a man without a mask, it's because he shows up with bad intentions—intentions he hides. Someone who cheats.

LITERATURE BY EVERYONE

Whenever language is at stake, it's wiser (and also more pleasant) to prefer the Port-au-Foin, the Halles, or a simple bistro, to polite society or evenings at home. When the public invents a word, that word is usually pleasant and tasty: it's *coudée* or *mal des ardents*. When experts or semiexperts invent a word, that word is absurd and poorly fabricated: it's *kilo,* or *eczema*. It's even *curozema,*[7] and *cosmogeopedomicrophysicozema* (a remedy for eczema discovered

7. "A specific remedy for dermatoses," says the prospectus.

by the inventor of *cosmogeopedomicrophysics*[8]). Everyone knows this; but I wonder if they notice another equally strange fact, or digest it well. In effect, everything happens as if the difficulty, and precisely the mystery, of the simplest language—where intellectuals and experts trip themselves up (along with the inventors of schools ending in *-ist*)—never posed any problem for the common man, the man of the street, the Modest Man, the man who works at winning his bread (he would gladly give up working), who raises his parakeets, plays horsey with his kids, and likes to hear the water slapping at his nice little boat on Sundays.

It doesn't trouble him at all. But that's the least of it; it interests him, it amuses him. I see celebrated authors who, whenever they write about problems (specialized, they think) of orthography or punctuation, are amazed at receiving two or three thousand letters, not only from retired judges, but from clerks and gardeners as well (who'd never be bothered by articles on social issues, or even philosophy). But they're wrong to be amazed: at stake is something very curious, even bewildering; a metamorphosis, a mystery in plain daylight; a word that is *also* a kind of dream, a letter that *becomes* an imagining. And as long as you stay naive, you won't keep that mystery from happening, or stop being astonished by it: sending words into the air, watching them turn into thoughts. Little pieces of words, even—an accent mark, or a single letter.

Literature isn't a specialty.

My point is that literature is a language too, and that (while not always seeming so) it's also a festival for everyone, where everyone's invited. It's not like pyrography on the bark of a willow-tree, or embroidery on tarlatan—something best shunned if we don't know how. It's more like love or dancing—something best done even when we don't yet know how to do it very well.

Only it's a festival, for the moment, that's rather slow at getting started: it's a language that's severely confused, that doesn't know quite what to say, or what saints to pray to, sometimes restricting itself to a thin little thread of finely chosen words and sometimes letting them all drop pell-mell in a waterfall over our heads. So why not, once again, consult with that Modest Man? Writers are hon-

8. This inventor is M. R. Vandelanotte, in Menin (Belgium).

est; they want the world to have beautiful poems and exciting stories. They don't always insist that these have to be theirs only, and indeed they can see very well—even the proudest—that inventing with feeling is better than imitating and combining by formula; that it's more amusing; that it resembles, as in the festival mentioned above, a sudden explosion or a fireworks display. So they should let this honest man of the street talk for a while, having only his feelings as a guide—above all without giving him the slightest program in advance! Without inviting him to be a realist or a surrealist (he would promptly obey, he's very suggestible)—and interrupting him (but then energetically) only when he starts to sound far too correct, in the style of the higher grades of an elementary school, in the familiar Bossuet style.

Minor fireworks.

What good is literature for everyday life? And who writes poetry today, say, for pleasure? Not for glory, which only serves his loves or his fantasies. This would be fascinating to find out. Yes, you'd pick up a few platitudes along the way—along with some baroque flourishes. But then you'd quickly find out that those baroque flourishes are full of sense and reason. And where the semiexpert is annoyed at hearing his concierge say *estatue,* the true expert, agreeing with the Modest Man, considers *estatue* to be an excellent French word and sees no good reason for saying *statue,* since we also say *escalier, escalade, estampiller, échelle.* (He continues to say *statue,* however, out of modesty on his part.)

It's not my point that we don't learn anything in polite society.

THE BENEFITS OF FAMILY GET-TOGETHERS

At a family get-together, celebrating the fifteenth birthday of some cousin or other, an unknown parent comes up and accosts me with lofty ideas: about the schooling of the young (we should warn them a year in advance, he says, about projects being planned for them); about the immorality now flourishing, alas!, in our time; particu-

Where the author meets a moralist.

larly among boys; more particularly in the sixth grade: most particularly in the sixth grade of the Condorcet school. As for me, I try to keep up the tone. And then we part.

Gossip shared, he proves to be the only smuggler in a family—my own—which on the whole is more or less honest and even, in some of its branches, almost exacting. You'd say that he lies. Not true: it's just that he probably feels, more keenly than anyone else, and quite rightly so, a need for morality.

It's the same with writers. I notice that we tend nowadays to blame one or another writer—a Sartre, say, or a Zola—for the filth, the mud-bath, in which he starts off by plunging his heroes. I, for one, would be more worried about the heavy moral lifting required to pull them out. *L'Assommoir* certainly has its greatness, but it has its failings too, especially when it invokes enfeebled *Work,* oppressive *Fecundity.*

In the midst of this little party, I began to play bridge again. This allowed me to make two or three findings, rather alarming ones.

II

From Bridge Enthusiasts to Volunteer Police

A DEVELOPING LANGUAGE

Shifting from auction to contract, the language of bridge was perfected almost as much as when shifting from whist to auction. A player today can spell out the details of his hand in four or five bids, to the point that bids are now made for little slams or grand slams. We prefer a sign-system in which, for example, "five clubs" no longer designates clubs but means instead: "I have no aces"; "six hearts": "I have three kings"; and so on. The verbal equivalent, then, of those finger (or piano) signals used by "truants" in the Latin Quarter to alert one another about their cards.

Fine. Anything beats a piano. But bear in mind that games are based mainly on elements of chance and invention, hypotheses; in a word, on wit. As soon as its language becomes perfect, bridge will become a precise calculus. You'll end up playing with your cards spread out on the table—and I've already pointed out that contract is more automatic and less amusing than auction.

A defect in international languages.

So too with international languages. You may be surprised to see them evaporate—Volapück, Esperanto, Ido, and the rest, one after the other. But the cause is obvious: their inventors decided from the start to make them perfect: each word refers to an object, and to one object only. But what attracts us to any language and makes us want to speak it is not its perfection. Rather, its confusion, its errors, its baroque flourishes.[1] Because any given word, by accident (by etymology or pun), can evoke twenty other words. In short, because it can stimulate the mind. But languages are ruined by an excess of precision.

There's something even more serious.

ANOTHER CAUSE FOR ALARM

In the old bridge, good and bad came at a single price: one trick over the bid was a hundred points won; one trick under, a hundred points lost.

The Beaulieu scoring system already started to change this. Failure became more serious, more spectacular than success (or good luck): only fifty points for getting more than your bid, a hundred for getting less. This was perhaps an effect of modern philosophy, a somber thing, as I've already mentioned.

But in contract, disappointment runs much deeper. One trick over counts for just twenty or thirty points in a given case, usually nothing at all; one trick under is suddenly one hundred, two hundred, three hundred points lost. In short, the game's language has reached a level of such perfection that the player is no less at fault—and ought to be no less disappointed—for having expected too little from his play than too much. And here we should also note that a perfect language admits of greater disappointment than hope, more penalties than rewards.

We prefer rewards.

Which is another reason, no doubt, for dropping perfect languages so quickly: we have a weakness for preferring lucky surprises and rewards. And I don't give contract ten years to survive. As for going back to auction, the likelihood of doing so is slight. In the

1. Certainly Esperanto, Volapück, and Ido are not perfect. But we can ruin them by deciding to *take* them as perfect. And an Esperantist indulging in puns is considered suspect.

first place, it would involve changing our ideas about language. And auction has also always had some drawbacks of its own: notably the bid for an (American) club, which pretty much meant: I have something of everything but clubs; *a counter* (also American), which said to one's partner: "Speak up, then! I'll give you some help": a certain value for points assigned to the first bid, and various other procedures already preparing the way for contract.

That last is a more general point.

CURIOUS CHATTER

In another respect, contract, like auction, strikes me as an occasion for painful misunderstanding. When players confine themselves to declaring (dryly): "A spade—I pass—no-trump . . .," there's nothing more to say. The problem is that they never fail to add, for instance:

> I PASS FOR NOW.
> I SAY ONE DIAMOND, MODESTLY.
> I WON'T COUNTER, OUT OF THE SHEER GOODNESS OF MY SOUL.
> BRIDGE MEANS SILENCE (something anyway not true[2]).
>
> YOU PLAYED LIKE A DEAD BRIDGE (or A DEAD FOOT, or A DEAD BALLOT, according to the idiom).
>
> FIVE THOUSAND ENGLISHMEN (or TWENTY THOUSAND, or A HUNDRED THOUSAND) HAVE DROWNED IN THE THAMES FOR NOT PLAYING TRUMP.
>
> THERE ARE TWO METHODS. (It seems the rule to add, moments later:) THE GOOD AND THE BAD.

Of course this could simply be a case of cheating—like the frowns, smiles, and grimaces that players use now and then to sharpen their bids. (In families, anyway, because families, in such moments, learn not to complain.)

But I'm only interested in moments when those little jests arise in all innocence. What happens then is this.

2. Here again we see the inconvenience of foreign words.

A PAINFUL MISUNDERSTANDING

The player who does the chattering (me, from time to time) can't contain his glee. He says to himself, more or less: "Ah, ha! That's not bad! That's clever." He has the delicious impression of talking to himself, with no great need for words. He's ineffable, but he follows himself very well. What fun! He glides through his mind, he flies over vowels, consonants, words, and sentences. Let him fly!

Fine. But the other player, hearing him, says to himself, on the contrary: "Play then, and shut up! Don't be so smart . . . Still more of his words, his gestures, his bluffs. You're hounding me. I was waiting for that." (This, this is the worst: nothing seems more contemptible, more *sententious,* than the sentence you were expecting.)

"And so what?" you ask. Well, it strikes me as a total disaster. How? If you said "flea," and your neighbor understood "elephant," or if you said "river," and he understood "acacia," you'd accuse him of incomprehension! (Though there are still some links between fleas and elephants.) But you're talking things, and he hears words! You're talking nuances, intimate thoughts, delicate feelings, and he hears vowels, consonants, sentences, words. Just when your language strikes you as perfect, he finds it completely hateful. Or even worse. Worse because appalling.

I'd rather not dwell on a topic so painful.

Our little family get-together ended without further incident. But there was a question of morality . . .

OF A SUPPLEMENTARY POLICE FORCE

Men of letters, I notice, haven't renounced this for a while now. (I don't mean popular writers, who were discussed elsewhere, but the clan of more or less professional writers I belong to.) They deserve to be praised, moralists were in short supply. But I think they might be a little clumsy, like any neophyte. (It's their debut.) Especially in applied morality. For example, at the National Committee of Writers (or, as they call it: the Céné), they've drawn up a list of guilty authors.

We don't lack for guilty writers.

This is not, in principle, a bad idea; we've never lacked for guilty writers: swindlers, counterfeiters, assassins, or simply bad men, worthless finally, ah no!: from Villon to Jean Genet, by way of Leibniz, Racine, Sade, Verlaine. And then there's Rimbaud (who wanted to see the Ardennes squeezed by the Germans)! Even Baudelaire, if so consumed by remorse, certainly must have had some reasons. I have in mind, then, the good, the true writers. And if literature is precisely a festival, no one would want it to take place without risks. It's a festival where a bomb blows up in your face, and that can end up (like any real festival) with the slashings of a knife. We might even ask whether guilt doesn't improve a writer—whether it doesn't comprise a part of literature, whether we don't have an interest in quickly becoming guilty, and whether we shouldn't invite the writer, once and for all, into error and madness. Because, finally, he takes chances for all of us, who have placed him at the farthest reaches of exploration and disquietude. (But then we promptly suppose that there must have been any number of writers who were even guiltier and whom we all forgot about.)

The guilty, all of them, have or have not been punished, such is the task of Justice—for finally it also goes with the game that constables interrupt it from time to time, precisely when it comes to the slashings of a knife. But never before (unless I'm mistaken) have we seen them denounced by their colleagues—by the "white," the respectable writers. Not without errors of detail, I fear. But the errors don't matter much, it's the principle of the thing that bothers me. It doesn't fail to alarm me. I have great respect for judges and policemen. I suppose they're necessary, I've even come to admire them (I don't belong to those anarchists who would want writers exempted from every law). But finally, I'm not one of them. No. Nor a politician. I lack the necessary qualities—along with the defects, I believe. The conscience of humanity (as the Céné calls it) isn't my thing. Any more than the supplementary police force that Charles Maurras demanded so loudly—the one you've found.

You found it. But were you looking for it?

THE WAYS OF WEAKNESS ARE NOT FORESEEN

I'm not so sure. When you said, for example, in the enthusiasm of the Liberation: "I shall never again write on the side of M. de Châteaubriant," you meant—or at least I thought you meant: "I know very well, in a rather feeble and lazy society—our own, the one between the wars—that M. de Châteaubriant, sworn traitor though he be, will recover his standing some day. Fine for him. Fine for them. You just won't find me working on their side." It was a courageous and modest decision; in a word (as we say nowadays), democratic.

The ways of weakness are not foreseen. From one day to the next, it isn't just one or two newspapers, it's the entire press, it's editorial houses and reviews closed to writers who've been blackened, thanks to your efforts. When we receive a novel by Céline, it reaches us from the equator; an essay by Marcel Jouhandeau, from Switzerland; a novel by Drieu la Rochelle, from Argentina. And merely to know what Gabriel Marcel thinks of the purge (he thinks ill of it), we have to go all the way to Canada. There has occurred a kind of (minor) revocation of the Edict of Nantes. I mean that your modest decision has turned, through human malice, into a pretentious verdict: your democratic measure, into a fascist sentence. Who would follow you there? We may have said at one time, lightly, that silence and an enforced period of reflection were good for authors. Fine, and I wouldn't let myself feel sorry for them. But for their readers? This is you, this is I, this is the man in the street who never stopped having the right to read the writers you censor; because, finally, I don't want to bother anyone (myself included). But it's a fact that we miss them.

The malice of men.

We miss them, and it shows. Ah, I wish I were a Jew, so that I could say—with more authority than I have—that I forgive France, once and for all, for having failed to defend me. I wish I were a Jew, so that I could work—with more force than I have—at giving France all its voices, its whole voice. I wish I were a Jew, so that I could become the best of the French.

ANTIPATRIOTS, A LUXURY FOR HOMELANDS

And by what right, then, do you judge? In the name of what principles? Truly, I see only one you might have in common.

You came to the Céné from many parties: communist, socialist, moderate, reactionary—but all of you guided, I think, by a common love for the homeland. It's a subtle rule, a love hard to handle.

In the first place, I notice that the homeland isn't accustomed to being as rancorous as you take it to be. It willingly forgets. We might even say that it's pleased to forget (maybe it's wrong). Romain Rolland himself, in '14, certainly betrayed the cause of France: he signalled from Switzerland, at the start of our thirty years' war, that he was refusing to choose between France and its aggressor. And for us, the danger was even greater at the time, because Rolland's honesty was more obvious, his disciples more numerous. But by '20 we all would have pardoned him, and who among us would have refused to write on his side? Because of that very honesty (which also made him more dangerous). Because of that obvious good faith. And to anyone who might have said to us: "But he betrayed our cause," we would have gladly replied (like a child scolded for breaking a vase): "But that was five years ago!"

The patriot is without rancor.

And then we thought that a country gave proof of its strength and health by making fun of its opponents this way. We've always been proud, and not without reason, of the French who were rather inclined to abuse France: Voltaire, Stendhal, Baudelaire, the Surrealists. Countries shouldn't be too smug. Fishermen ask God for enough fish to let them steal a few, and patriots ask France for enough French to keep a few enemies around. Bad patriots—a luxury for homelands. (Dangerous, like any luxury.) And besides . . .

Here I was violently interrupted.

III

Seven Letters to White Writers

OF A CERTAIN RIGHT TO ERROR

Dear friends,

You find me completely surprised by the venture. My colleagues never stopped saying: "Oh, come on! What does the Céné defend? Freedom of thought. That's article five of the charter. Go look!"

Poor me, I was a bit dubious. I certainly saw another article in the charter, where members of the Céné swear never to forsake "the principles that carried France to the forefront of nations." France at the forefront of nations flatters me. But what the principles were, the charter never said. I finally collected my courage. What did I say? More or less: "I seem to find a few on your blacklist who might be less guilty than a Rimbaud, a Romain Rolland . . ." I said this, in fact, to gather evidence for my side. As if to say: "As true as two and two makes four . . ." Ah, did I score!

Along comes a newspaper to report this little idea. Promptly a great uproar. I'm hit with an open letter—very stirring, very stirred—signed by sixteen good authors who implore me—politely, by the way—to change my mind; from *Gavroche* to *The Marseillaise*, twenty ripostes; a special page in the *Lettres Françaises*, which buries me in fifty studies, citations, memories, anecdotes, anonymous items; a commemorative evening at the Sorbonne devoted to the glory of Rolland; an intervention, before a plenary Congress in Strasbourg, by the Communist Party's director in charge of literature (his name is Casanova). A discussion is held at a meeting of the Directors' Committee as to whether I shouldn't be blacklisted myself. Right down to the very newspaper where my little idea first appeared, and which hastens to disown me.

Everyone's apt to think I get more attention than I deserve. And yes, I definitely agree. But we still have to admit, finally, that it's all very curious in a funny way, all this fuss over something so minor. There's certainly something about me going on here . . . So whom did I upset? What happened? What principle might I have violated?

I'm right—that's the problem. It has to be said this isn't fun. Personally, I was concerned with something else entirely. To my mind, an author has a perfect right to be wrong (even about Romain Rolland); to be at risk, risky. He isn't a priest or a sage, after all. Risk is a big part of every work from his hand; you have to throw yourself into writing, otherwise you'd never write. I've seen more than one of the best of them working away like an artisan, building by fits and starts, correcting endlessly, growing from error to error. And then he's expected to hold forth every day on a thousand topics he lacks the time to explore: the structure of the state, love, the atom bomb, not to mention the human condition itself. Even if he tries to keep his thoughts to himself, the reader goes straight to the point. What room for error, and what courage it takes to write!

A writer isn't a sage.

At least you can see what I was getting at: slipping a little article into the Céné's charter, granting the author a right to errors. I would gladly have offered myself as an example (those are the best examples). But it's too late now. Alas, as it turns out, I'm right. And so I'll defend myself, as best I can.

THE ROMAIN ROLLAND MISTAKE

Just between us, if I'd been wrong, you wouldn't have needed sixteen. Less than one would have been enough: an anonymous item, like the one I find at the bottom of the page. But you needed sixteen, and no less, I suspect, to claim that *Above the Battle* doesn't mean: above the battle. That's what's called argument from authority. How to conceal the fact that I'm not very impressed?

Rolland's whole thesis consists in saying that though the Germans were certainly guilty in 1914, the French were hardly innocent. When he writes:

> THE HEADS OF STATE, WHO, TO MY KNOWLEDGE, ARE THE CRIMINAL AUTHORS OF THESE WARS, DON'T DARE ACCEPT RESPONSIBILITY; EVERY ONE OF THEM TRIES, UNDERHANDEDLY, TO SHIFT THE BLAME TO HIS OPPONENT. AND THE PEOPLE WHO TAMELY FOLLOW ARE RESIGNED . . . (p. 25)

it's as much about the French as the Germans. It's as much about Poincaré as Sazonov or Wilhelm. When he adds:

> LET EACH DECLARE HIS OWN MEA CULPA NOW! THIS INTELLECTUAL ELITE, THESE CHURCHES, THESE WORKER PARTIES NEVER WANTED WAR . . . FINE! WHAT DID THEY DO TO PREVENT IT? WHAT DID THEY DO TO LIMIT IT? THEY'RE SETTING THE FIRE. EACH OF THEM BRINGS HIS OWN KINDLING. (p. 26)

it's as much about French socialists as German socialists. When he adds:

> EVERY COUNTRY MORE OR LESS HAS ITS OWN IMPERIALISM; BE IT MILITARY, FINANCIAL, FEUDAL, *republican*, SOCIAL OR INTELLECTUAL IN FORM, IT'S A BLOOD-SUCKER SUCKING THE FINEST BLOOD IN EUROPE. (p. 33)

I'm certainly supposed to recall that France, of the five countries at war, was the one and only republic. Moreover, Rolland repeats:

> THERE'S NOT A GOVERNMENT TODAY THAT DOESN'T TREMBLE BEFORE PUBLIC OPINION . . . NOTHING SHOWED THIS BETTER THAN EFFORTS ON BOTH SIDES, WITH THEIR MINISTERS, CHANCELLORS AND SOVEREIGNS, TO JUSTIFY THEIR OWN CRIMES BE-

FORE AN INVISIBLE COURT OF THE HUMAN RACE, AND DENOUNCE THE CRIMES OF THEIR ADVERSARIES. (p. 35)

What crimes, then, has France committed?

To justify *their own* crimes, as you certainly read. As for what the crimes of France might have been in 1914, Romain Rolland doesn't try to explain. I think he would have found it hard to do so. (Fabre-Luce also tried later on, with no great success.)

I limit myself to recalling a few texts—without them we'd never grasp the fury aroused by *Above the Battle*, the indignation—not, I should say, of Maurras or Massis alone, but of good democrats with names like Andler and Verhaeren. Benda wrote to Rolland:

> A WORD OF PRAISE FOR THE DEFENDERS OF LIEGE AND LOUVAIN? QUICKLY THE SAME FOR THOSE DEFENDING THE "CITY OF KANT," NOT NOTICING THAT THE FIRST ARE DEFENDING THEMSELVES AGAINST THOSE *attacking* THEM, AND THE OTHERS AGAINST THOSE *they attacked.* DO YOU DEPLORE THE GERMAN INCURSION INTO BELGIUM? YOU PROMPTLY DEPLORE THE RUSSIANS IN POMERANIA, DETERMINED TO OVERLOOK THE FACT THAT ONE IS AN OUTRAGE AGAINST LAW, WHERE THE OTHER IS MERELY AN ACT OF WAR. DO YOU DENOUNCE INTELLECTUALS IN GERMANY? PROMPTLY A SLAP ON THE WRIST AGAINST OUR SIDE, CHOOSING TO IGNORE THE FACT THAT THE FIRST ARE WRONG, WHILE MANY OF THE OTHERS ARE RIGHT.[1]

Gabriel Séailles:

> IT WAS YOUR OWN BAD LUCK, ROMAIN ROLLAND, NOT TO HAVE DROWNED IN A FLOOD OF OUR PEOPLE ON THE DAY YOU LEFT.[2]

The historian Alphonse Aulard:

> WITH ROLLAND'S HELP, A GERMAN MANEUVER SWEEPS ACROSS ALL OF EUROPE.[3]

And in fact the defeatists of the time weren't wrong on this point—the Pierre Lavals and Guilbeaux who turned Rolland into their flag.[4]

But you cite me some other texts that are troubling even today.

---

1. *Les Sentiments de Critias,* pp. 269 ff.
2. *La Guerre Sociale,* p. 9. I, 1915.
3. *L'Intransigeant,* 6 March 1915.
4. Pierre Laval discovered how to be a defeatist in two wars: he was a revolutionary in 1914, and a reactionary in 1940.

Yes, it's true that Rolland writes, a little further on:

> ...WHO DROVE THE PEOPLE TO WAR IF NOT THEIR STATES, AND UPPERMOST (TO MY MIND) THE THREE GREAT GUILTY STATES, THE THREE RAPACIOUS EAGLES, THE THREE EMPIRES, THE TORTUOUS POLITICS OF THE HOUSE OF AUSTRIA, VORACIOUS TSARISM AND BRUTAL PRUSSIA?

(But famished tsarism was our ally, and for good or ill we defended it too. But here's something more serious:)

> . . . THE GREATEST DANGER FOR US MEN IN THE WEST, THE THREAT HANGING OVER THE HEAD OF EUROPE THAT FORCES US TO UNITE IN ITS DEFENSE, IS PRUSSIAN IMPERIALISM, THE EXPRESSION OF A MILITARY AND FEUDAL CASTE, A FLAIL, NOT JUST FOR THE REST OF THE WORLD, BUT ALSO FOR GERMANY, WHOSE MIND IT SO DELIBERATELY POISONED. THIS HAS TO BE DESTROYED FROM THE START . . .

> . . . FREEDOM'S GREATEST ENEMY, A DESPOTISM THREATENING EVERYONE—THE FRENCH, THE ENGLISH, AND WESTERN MAN—IS PRUSSIAN IMPERIALISM; AND I SEE THE CHRONICLE OF ITS CAMPAIGN WRITTEN ALONG THE DEVASTATED ROAD FROM LIEGE TO SENLIS, THROUGH LOUVAIN, MALINES AND REIMS.

Of a curious contradiction.

which all seems to show that Rolland didn't just hold the heads of state responsible—"Not all of them," you say, "or not to the same degree." And I can certainly see that if my opinion is plausible, yours is hardly less so. Who shall decide between us?

It happens, as a matter of fact, that Romain Rolland stood self-accused of all these charges. To Bachelin, who sketched out a defense of *Above the Battle* in 1921 rather like your own, he answers:

> THE CHARACTER PRESUMED TO REPRESENT MY THOUGHT, LAGARDE, DEFENDS IT WITH EXTREME TIMIDITY, AND HE CERTAINLY DOESN'T UNDERSTAND IT. IN *Above the Battle,* I SAID THE MAXIMUM OF WHAT I COULD SAY PUBLICLY IN FRANCE AT THE TIME (OR IN THE SWISS ROMANDE—FOR THEY WERE ONE AND THE SAME: THE SWISS ROMANDE WAS AN ARM OF THE FRENCH WAR PROPAGANDA MACHINE). BUT THAT MAXIMUM WAS *the minimum of what I thought.* NEITHER MATERIALLY NOR MORALLY COULD I SAY ANYTHING MORE AT THE TIME. MATERIALLY, BECAUSE IT WOULD NOT HAVE BEEN PUBLISHED. MORALLY, BECAUSE THE INDIGNATION THAT MY WORDS MIGHT HAVE IN-

SPIRED WOULD HAVE LED TO THE VAIN SACRIFICES OF TRAGIC MUTINIES, OR INCREASED THEIR AGONY.

You, Martin-Chauffier, dare to tell me that "Romain Rolland fled France, my God, like Bernanos, Maritain and General de Gaulle, to speak and act freely."[5] Fine. But the freedom of Bernanos, Maritain and de Gaulle reinforced France's defenders. Rolland's freedom—by Rolland's own admission—drove them to despair.

Romain Rolland continues:

IN TRUTH, I DON'T CONDEMN GERMANY ANY MORE THAN FRANCE. I CONDEMN GERMANY AND FRANCE, ENGLAND AND RUSSIA . . . I BELIEVE IN THE ENORMOUS REPONSIBILITIES OF THE FRENCH GOVERNMENT. AND OF THE ENGLISH AND RUSSIAN GOVERNMENTS AS WELL (NO LESS THAN THOSE OF THE GERMANS). THE ONLY DIFFERENCE BETWEEN THEM IS ONE OF SKILL; AND THE MOST SKILLFUL WERE THOSE WITH THE OLDEST TRADITIONS IN GRAND DIPLOMACY—THE MEN IN THE FOREIGN OFFICE.

Wherein Rolland undertakes to explain the contradiction.

So the answer is obvious. Benda and Séailles, Aulard and Andler—Maurras and Massis, alas—got it right. You're the ones who got it wrong, the dupes of artifice and oratorical precaution.

Romain Rolland concludes:

. . . IT'S MY ABSOLUTE CONVICTION THAT THE TRUE OBJECT (DEEP, NOT ADMITTED) OF THE WAR OF 1914–1918 WAS TO DESTROY THE NATION WORKING HARDEST, FOR THE BENEFIT OF NATIONS THAT WORKED THE LEAST, ESPECIALLY ENGLAND. THIS IS A CRIME AGAINST THE INTERESTS OF HUMANITY. ENGLAND WILL PAY.[6]

Rolland thought this, wrote this when France, invaded twice in forty-five years, was already marshalling its forces—and trying to enlist the world's—against a third invasion. You've noticed the two themes of pan-Germanic propaganda soon to be echoed by Hitler: that Germany is under attack, and that Germany, the envy of Europe, is the land of righteousness and work. Does it now seem unfair or inaccurate to say that Romain Rolland, himself French,

5. *Les Lettres Françaises,* 22 January 1947.
6. *Lettre à Bachelin,* 9 April 1921. Cf. Catalogue Charavay, no. 672.

thereby betrayed the cause of France? He condemns the cause of France, he calls it a "crime." What more do you need?

Romain Rolland's great honesty, you tell me . . .—No doubt.— And then the cause of the bourgeois Republic wasn't so pure.— Fine.—Poincaré dreamed of revenge.—Maybe.—And anyway, what are you getting at?—Ah, I have no idea. Perhaps it was right (but I don't believe it) to betray the cause of France in 1914. I'm saying that Romain Rolland did betray it. I've always been told that we have to tell the truth, at whatever the cost. I'm telling the truth. As for costs, we've already seen a few. Furthermore, I bear no resentment at all toward Rolland. But I have the vague idea that the truth itself might be at stake in a world where error, in self-defense, so readily piles up open letters on commemorations at the Sorbonne, and gossip on top of lies.

THE RIMBAUD LIE

I have no taste for polemics. I don't write pamphlets. When I talk about lying, with regard to the items that Louis Aragon sent to the *Lettres Françaises,* don't suppose that I'm furious, or merely annoyed. I try to see things clearly.

I happened to recall that Rimbaud wanted to see the Ardennes squeezed by our enemy. This was news to no one. But Aragon makes this reply:

> IT WILL BE NOTED THAT THE BASIS OF THIS ALLEGATION IS A PROPOSAL BY RIMBAUD IN A PRIVATE LETTER TO A FRIEND IN 1873, TWO YEARS AFTER THE END OF THE WAR OF 1870–1871. IT WILL BE NOTED THAT THIS PROPOSAL IS AN EXPRESSION OF RIMBAUD'S RAGE AGAINST THOSE WHO, WITH THE COMPLICITY OF BISMARCK, HAD JUST MASSACRED FRENCH PATRIOTS IN PARIS—THOSE MEN OF THE COMMUNE WHO SOUGHT TO PURSUE A WAR AGAINST THE INVADER, AND WHOSE FIGHTING RIMBAUD EXTOLLED. IT WILL THEN BE NOTED, NECESSARILY, THAT PAULHAN, ON THE BASIS OF THIS FACT, TRIES, WHEN AC-

> CUSING RIMBAUD, TO WHITEWASH THE VERSAILLAIS UNDER THIERS.[7]

I won't go very far to seek my support.

On 23 October 1927, Charleville dedicated a monument to Rimbaud. On that occasion, deputies, mayors, and municipal counsellors from the Ardennes received a four-page tract: *Permit . . .*, addressed to them as an open letter:

Rimbaud, or defeatism in wartime.

> WE ARE CURIOUS TO KNOW HOW YOU COULD RECONCILE THE TOWN'S MONUMENT HONORING THOSE WHO DIED FOR THEIR COUNTRY, WITH A MONUMENT COMMEMORATING A MAN WHO EMBODIES THE LOFTIEST CONCEPT OF DEFEATISM, AN ACTIVE DEFEATISM THAT YOU SENT TO THE FIRING-SQUAD DURING THE WAR. YOU MUST ADMIT, GENTLEMEN, THAT THIS CHANCE TO GO MAD WITH PATRIOTISM IS PERHAPS POORLY CHOSEN, SINCE THE PERSON YOU CELEBRATE WOULD ONLY SALUTE YOU WITH GESTURES OF OPEN DISGUST, AND WITH WORDS OF HATE, AND WOULD ONLY ENJOY A GLORY COMPLETELY AT ODDS WITH THE GLORY OF WRITERS DYING FOR FRANCE . . .

Here the manifesto cites, not without praise, various texts by Rimbaud:

> HOW CREEPY, THOSE RETIRED GROCERS DECKED OUT IN UNIFORM! IT'S STUNNING HOW SEXY IT IS, NOTARIES, GLAZIERS, TEACHERS AND ALL THOSE BELLIES WITH RIFLES AT THEIR CHESTS, DOING THEIR PATRIDIOTIC THING IN FRONT OF THE GATES OF MÉZIERES. MY COUNTRY RISES UP! ME, I'D RATHER SEE IT SEATED! . . . (25 August 1870)

> SNIPERY HERE AND THERE. A DESTESTABLE RASH OF IDIOCY, SUCH IS THE SPIRIT OF THE POPULATION. (2 Nov. 1870)

> I REALLY HOPE THE ARDENNES WILL BE OCCUPIED AND SQUEEZED TIGHTER AND TIGHTER. (June 1872)

> TWO DAYS AGO I WENT TO SEE THE PRUSSIANS AT VOUZIERS, A SUB-PREFECTURE OF 10,000 SOULS, SEVEN KILOM. FROM HERE. IT REVIVED ME. (May 1873)

In 1873 France suffered—as it would after 1940—an occupation by the Germans. The Commune had been wiped out two years

---

7. *Les Lettres Françaises,* 14 February 1947.

earlier. Rimbaud's attitude finally expresses nothing more than his rage against the French.

On this topic, the tract says something more:

> FRANCE IN EVERY WAY DISGUSTED HIM. ITS SPIRIT, ITS GREAT MEN, ITS CUSTOMS AND ITS LAWS SYMBOLIZED FOR HIM EVERYTHING IN THE WORLD THAT WAS LOWEST AND MOST TRIVIAL:
>
> "WHAT A HORROR, THIS FRENCH CAMPAIGN . . . WHAT CRAP! . . . EVERYTHING IS FRENCH, MEANING THAT IT'S HATEFUL TO THE UTMOST DEGREE; FRENCH, NOT PARISIAN! JUST ANOTHER WORK BY THE ODIOUS GENIUS INSPIRING RABELAIS, VOLTAIRE, JEAN DE LA FONTAINE! . . ."

France disgusted him.

And still further:

> PERHAPS THE STATUE UNVEILED TODAY WILL SUFFER THE SAME FATE AS THE ONE BEFORE IT.[8] THAT STATUE, CAPTURED BY THE GERMANS, WAS UNDOUBTEDLY MELTED DOWN FOR ARTILLERY SHELLS, AND RIMBAUD WOULD HAVE RELISHED THE PROSPECT OF WATCHING ONE OF THEM FLATTEN YOUR *PLACE DE LA GARE* FROM END TO END . . .

You'll find it singular, then, that Aragon should mistake his authors on this point and be ignorant of history.

He isn't ignorant of history. Here's the really curious fact: the manifesto *Permit* . . . bears the signature of Aragon.

If, then, Aragon is deceived today, he'd be the first to know he's deceived. He expressly deceives himself. When he accuses me of "whitewashing the Versaillais under Thiers" (*sic*) he knows very well he lies. An odd lie: naive, because quite a few of us still read Rimbaud; impudent, because the tract itself can still be found in libraries. Does he hold his readers in such contempt that he hopes to persuade them with tricks that Cadum soap wouldn't use for its publicity—or the police for their investigations?

Someone will now argue that Aragon is an old hand at these tricks. That a lie never bothers him. Sartre caught him, in flagrante delicto, in an act of slander the other day. And what a slander! It was an attempt to disgrace the writer Nizan, who died for France.[9] Paul Eluard speaks of Aragon's double game, his compromises, his

Curious lies by Aragon.

8. It did in fact suffer it.

9. *Les Temps Modernes*, n. 22.

"bad faith masked in sentimental blackmail," the "endless repudiations from which he draws all his energy," his "arrivism, which finds its natural nourishment in denial."[10] And a lot of other things as well. (Who was it, finally, who called him the *Liar of Castile*?)

But the Rimbaud lie, like the Rolland error, poses some problems that go far beyond the case of Aragon.

THE LIARS CASSOU, VERCORS, MARTIN-CHAUFFIER

I'm not a moralist. I don't know whether anyone has to be a patriot, and it's said that a lie can have its own raison d'être, indeed its own nobility. That's not my thing. I merely explore the rationale for a certain malaise I wasn't alone in feeling over the past three years; one I particularly felt, let me say, at the home of the C.N.E., though I rarely set foot there. I seek it—as a doctor would with lapses or failed acts—in lies, errors, and contradictions.

I proceed.

When I ask what principles you invoke when you judge and what your blacklist might mean, you give me two kinds of answers—the first one being unobjectionable, and apparently sincere, and in any case closed to discussion.

Closed, because it doesn't give rise to discussion. Thus Louis Martin-Chauffier:

> THIS MANIA TO REPRESENT US AS JUDGES, AGAINST OUR WILL AND DESPITE OUR CONDUCT, PROVES TROUBLING. WE MUST BE VERY INNOCENT INDEED IF, TO REPROACH US, THEY HAVE TO INVENT REPROACHES . . . WE AREN'T JUDGES. WE'RE JUST HONEST FOLK WHO INTEND TO CHOOSE OUR FRIENDS. THE WATERS PARTED IN 1940.[11]

10. *Certificat,* 1934.
11. *Les Lettres Françaises,* 22 January 1947.

How to reply? He has a right, certainly, to choose his friends. But Jean Cassou, in his noble modesty:

> WE ENDURE CROWDED CONDITIONS AND CLOSE QUARTERS WITH IMPATIENCE. HITLER DID US THE FAVOR OF HELPING US SET SOME LIMITS ON THIS MOB SCENE. AND YOU WOULD HAVE ME SURRENDER THE BENEFIT OF THOSE LIMITS! . . .
>
> I REMAIN TRUE TO THE IMPULSE THAT DROVE US. NO MORE THAN ANYONE ELSE HAVE I EVER FELT, OR WILL I EVER FEEL, THAT I HAVE THE MENTALITY OF A JUDGE. THE C.N.E. DOESN'T ASPIRE TO EXERCISE CONTROL OVER LITERARY LIFE. IT'S NEITHER A HOLY OFFICE NOR A COMMITTEE OF PUBLIC SAFETY. IT'S CONTENT TO BE A MEMORY.[12]

Are you judges?

Myself, I understand this very well. But I don't refrain, finally, from doubting the wisdom of depending on Hitler when trying to distinguish true from false friends. What if Hitler hadn't arrived? Again, Jean Cassou said recently that he felt more vexed than ever by importunate people. What next? Does he hope for a new Hitler?

As for Vercors:

> I DON'T JUDGE. I DON'T CONDEMN THEM OR PUNISH THEM—OR ACQUIT THEM. IF THEY FILL ME WITH DISGUST, THAT'S MY RIGHT, IF I'M NOT MISTAKEN. I REFUSE TO DINE WITH THEM: ISN'T THAT ALSO MY RIGHT? I'M FREE PERHAPS TO DINE WITH WHOM I LIKE, AM I NOT? TO CHOOSE MY FRIENDS? . . . THINKING ABOUT THEM MAKES ME SICK. WE ONLY WANT TO AVOID SEEING THEM, NOTHING MORE. BECAUSE THEY DISGUST US, THEY REVOLT US, THEIR PHYSIOGNOMY RUINS OUR APPETITE.[13]

Here's certainly someone open and direct. To call him right? This would wound him. In no way does he seek to be right. He tells us how he feels. I find him very congenial. Very agreeable. The sight of certain people makes him sick. So let him refuse to dine with them! No sensible person could wish for a sick Vercors. And I, who don't always feel exactly the same as he? Well, Vercors leaves it completely up to me. Those are his terms, he couldn't care less. What more do I want?

Vercors could care less.

Even so, isn't there something you might prefer, Vercors, to your

12. *Les Lettres Françaises,* 10 January 1947.
13. *Petit pamphlet des diners chez Gazette.*

feelings? Cassou, to your memories? Martin-Chauffier, to your good friends? Here, other answers are forthcoming.

Ah, these answers are very different from the first. They've been addressed to me in the name of the whole Céné. They have something rather imperial about them. Something solemn. I have to admit they remind me of certain ukases from Charles Maurras.

If I go back to the declaration of August '44:

> THE NATIONAL COMITTEE OF WRITERS DEMANDS THAT MEASURES BE TAKEN AGAINST:
>
> WRITERS WHO AGREED TO APPEAR AT VARIOUS CONGRESSES HELD IN GERMANY AFTER JUNE 1940.
>
> WRITERS WHO, WITH THEIR WRITINGS, THEIR DEEDS AND THEIR INFLUENCE HELPED, ENCOURAGED AND SUSTAINED HITLERIAN PROPAGANDA . . .
>
> THE NATIONAL COMMITTEE OF WRITERS WILL COOPERATE FULLY WITH THE GOVERNMENT SO AS TO PUT INTO ACTION THE MEASURES DEMANDED.

I'm told we were fighting total war at the time; that the Germans could have returned to Paris overnight; that it was a matter of preventing, as soon as possible, any harm that might be done by the friends of our enemies. Yes, it's all true. So don't claim you refuse to judge. Claim that you had, at the time, the most pressing of reasons for judging.—But everything's changed, you say.—Maybe so. But here's an answer, dated 22 November '46, sent to me by the same Céné whose presidents, unless I'm mistaken, are Martin-Chauffier and Cassou:

> FOR THOSE WHO MIGHT BE MISTAKEN, IT'S WELL TO RECALL THAT MORAL SANCTIONS TAKEN BY THE C.N.E., WHICH HAVE NO BEARING ON PERSONS OR GOODS, DIFFER AS WELL FROM JURIDICAL SANCTIONS BY VIRTUE OF THE FACT THAT, IN THE FACE OF AN IRREPARABLE CRIME OR IRREVERSIBLE INJURY DONE TO THE NATION, THEY HAVE NO STATUTE OF LIMITATIONS, UNLIKE JURIDICAL SANCTIONS. AND THERE ARE PEOPLE WHOM DEATH ITSELF CANNOT SAVE, WHO CAN PAY ONLY IN THE EYES OF JUSTICE, NOT IN THE EYES OF HUMAN CONSCIENCE.[14]

---

14. *Les Lettres Françaises,* 22 November 1946.

I beg the pardon of my friends at the Céné, but adopting eternal sanctions against an irreparable crime, and in the name of Human Conscience, is precisely what we call judging. It's the very model of judging. You couldn't do better.

Where the mystique becomes political.

Not that I harbor the slightest doubt about the sincerity of Vercors, Martin-Chauffier, or Jean Cassou. According to all the evidence, none of them wanted this. And so? So what happens next, and what, unknown to them, turns their feelings into eternal judgments, their memories into sanctions—their mystique into politics? Where did all those lies come from? By whom, or by what, were you fooled?

I shall pursue this.

OF A SINGULAR HYPOCRISY

I'm not a Politician. The fact that society and the world in general need changing is blindingly obvious. As for how to change them, I leave that to others more knowledgeable than I. It's not my concern. I only ask that Politicians settle for changing the world and not begin by changing the truth.

A purge makes life hard for writers. Engineers, entrepreneurs, and masons who built the Atlantic wall now move among us in utter tranquillity. They're busy building new walls. They could be building walls for new prisons—for journalists who made the mistake of writing that the Atlantic wall was built well.

Where writers make a fortune.

Here's how we men of letters made a fortune three years ago. I'm talking about a moral fortune. This was something new. Earlier, when a writer had given enough praise to crime or immorality, he was actually invited to join the Académie Française. He soon began to see things with a different eye; meanwhile his disciples were aging quietly in a labor camp.

But you changed all that: for you, the criminal seemed less guilty than the writer attracting him to the crime, the traitor more pardonable than the ideologue counselling treason. And so you chose to pursue the author instead of the player, the cause instead of the effect. This was not only new, it was also just and wise. In a world where uncertain Justice, spread between special juries, vague laws, and Petainist judges, had only the absurd resource of seeming implacable, we were finally prepared to take full responsibility.

—And from what could have come the extraordinary authority of the Céné; of the old master it chose for itself, Romain Rolland; of its poet, Paul Eluard; of its sharpshooter, Julian Benda; of its momentary presidents; of Aragon, its irremovable secretary? From what could have come the respect accorded its decisions? The virtue of the principles cited?

Or rather the principle: for up to now, as I've mentioned, I've seen only one of these. It's the homeland. It's something even less: it's the homeland in a raw state, long before any awareness of it, or any wish to belong to it, improve it, or defend it. In a word, the nation. The only complaint you lodged against the writers appearing on your blacklist has nothing to do with error, greed, baseness, or a taste for ruin, but with an "irreparable crime, an irreversible injury done to the nation."

Aragon, your general secretary, comes back to this point a hundred times. As when he claims, for example, that there's a "common reality above us, a force that bears us away, from which it's unthinkable that we could ever be separated, it's the history of France, it's France."[15] This seems clear and convincing. There are, however, malicious minds who might argue that wars so atrocious could never have happened without the almost mindless faith that various European peoples placed in their nation. I suspect a thousand other objections. I don't have to invent them, they've already been made.

They were not—a curious thing—always made by your enemies:

It isn't Châteaubriant who says that "in 1914, a free conscience took leave of that old, bleeding fetish, the Homeland":

> HOMELAND, WHY DID YOU BETRAY US? WHY THESE BATTLES? FOR OUR FREEDOM? YOU ENSLAVE US. FOR OUR CONSCIENCE? YOU SCANDALIZE IT. FOR OUR HAPPINESS? YOU RAVAGE IT.

---

15. *Les Lettres Françaises,* 5 July 1946.

No, it's Romain Rolland. He adds:

> WE GAVE UP OUR SONS. FINE FOR ANYONE WHO BELIEVES IN THAT VICIOUS, ENVIOUS OLD IDOL CAKED IN CLOTTED BLOOD—THE BARBARIC HOMELAND. BUT FOR THOSE WHO NO LONGER BELIEVE, THOSE WHO ONLY WANT TO BELIEVE (IT IS I! IT IS WE!) WHILE SACRIFICING THEIR SONS—THEY GIVE THEM UP TO A *lie*, THEY GIVE THEM UP TO PROVE THEIR *lie* TO THEMSELVES.[16]

(I think Rolland means: to prove to themselves that their lie was nothing of the kind.)

It isn't Maurras who gives the following advice to intellectuals:

> YOU SHOULD BE THE ONES TO BLUSH AT HAVING A NATION . . . WITH EVERYTHING IN YOUR POWER YOU SHOULD HEAP RIDICULE ON NATIONALIST FERVOR. SHOW HOW IT TURNS ITS DEVOTEES INTO VERITABLE PUPPETS, READY TO RECANT ANYTHING . . .

No. It's Julien Benda, who goes on to say:

> HAD THE HOHENSTAUFENS BEEN ABLE TO UNITE GERMANY AND ITALY, THE WORLD WOULD HAVE ENJOYED A BEAUTIFUL PEACE FOR CENTURIES ON END . . . NEVER AGAIN WILL WE SEE A MAN WHO DECIDES TO CONQUER EUROPE IN ORDER TO UNITE IT, TO MAKE IT HIS OWN.[17]

(But yes, in fact, we did see him again. Never despair.)

It isn't Lucien Rebatet who writes, concerning the dead of 1914:

> A NEW RELIGION WAS FOUNDED AFTER THE WAR; THE MOST ABSURD, THE UGLIEST RELIGION OF ALL: A RELIGION OF THE DEAD.
>
> AND OF WHAT DEAD! TO FIGHT, THEY HAD TO BE DRESSED UP IN LIVERY . . . SHAME ON THOSE FIGHTERS WATCHED BY POLICE. AND ABOVE ALL, SHAME ON THE DEAD, FOR THEY ARE BEYOND REDEMPTION.

No, it's Paul Eluard. And further on:

> DEAD SLAVES ARE STILL SLAVES. NOTHINGNESS . . . THERE ARE ONE MILLION FIVE HUNDRED THOUSAND DEAD, THERE ARE TEN MILLION DEAD, THERE ARE ONE BILLION FIVE HUNDRED MILLION DEAD . . . PEACE![18]

---

16. *Clérambault,* pp. 156, 159.
17. *Discours à la Nation Européenne,* 1933.
18. *La Révolution Surréaliste,* 15 October 1925.

(Since then we've found, in Eluard's own poems, a new religion of the dead.)

And it isn't, finally, Drieu la Rochelle who cries out:

> MORE THAN PATRIOTISM ITSELF, WHICH IS ONE HYSTERIA AMONG OTHERS, WHAT DISGUSTS US MOST IS THE IDEA OF THE HOMELAND, TRULY THE MOST BESTIAL, THE LEAST PHILOSOPHICAL CONCEPT OF ALL, WHERE THEY TRY TO INVADE OUR MIND.

No. You've recognized Aragon, who goes on to say:

> MY HOMELAND, WHICH I DETEST, WHERE I FIND EVERYTHING THAT IS FRENCH, LIKE MYSELF, DISGUSTING TO THE EXTENT THAT IT IS *French* . . . I TEAR MYSELF AWAY FROM A FRANCE THAT ONLY GAVE ME SOME LITTLE SONGS AND AN ASSASSIN'S BLUE UNIFORM . . . LAUGH ON, WE SHALL GIVE AID AND COMFORT TO THE ENEMY FOREVER.[19]

(Drieu la Rochelle wrote entirely otherwise. His weakness—his own, after displaying the greatest courage in 1914—his weakness undoubtedly lay in being haunted thereafter by his homeland, and, upon seeing it abandoned, reaching the brink of total despair.)

Here someone will say that no one ever expected more from Julien Benda than a survey from Sirius. Fine. But I also recognize ten authors who seem to have contemplated all the latest battles from Sirius, and to whom you have shown no mercy: Montherlant, Giono, Thérive. Someone will say that no one ever asked Paul Eluard for political advice. But yes! I saw Brasillach pay the closest attention to Eluard's political advice—Brasillach, whose own father was among the dead of '14. Someone will say that no one ever considered Romain Rolland to be a thinker. But yes! But yes! I know at least one man who looked upon Rolland as a great thinker (and *vice versa*): Châteaubriant himself, whom Rolland called his "younger brother in the name of glory." Someone will say that no one ever took Aragon seriously for an instant. But I know someone who indeed admired Aragon, and perhaps took him all too seriously: the unfortunate Drieu la Rochelle.

Understand me. I don't reproach you for having changed. I'm not about to imagine—in Rolland's words—that you suddenly

---

19. *La Revolution Surréaliste,* 15 October 1925.

turned so inflexible to validate your lie, or to impart the force of truth to some new creed. Your change has motives, of course; sincerity among them, I hope; but I fear the tricky nuance of the word *homeland.* Moreover, certain things happened during the last fifteen years that you were far from foreseeing. (But is a lack of foresight really a virtue? In the end, neither Drieu, nor Montherlant, nor Thérive foresaw, any more than anyone else, the horrors of the concentration camps and the gas chambers.)

We're among friends, I wouldn't wound any one of you. But let me repeat the question I posed at our first public meeting. I ask you, seeing you all so hot for the death of a Brasillach, or a Rebatet—furious, and talking with Claude Morgan about the "insult to our martyrs"[20] if a victim should happen to escape—I ask you whether you're free of the men you sent so easily to the firing squad. I see only too well how limited they were in profiting from the lessons that we on the left could give them. And I'd certainly want them to profit at an untimely moment. But those lessons were ours. Yet you never stop talking about memory, recollection, fidelity to the self. Hearing you, someone might think you'd just invented the responsibility of the writer . . . If I were a moralist or a politician, I suppose the cruelty of the purge would strike me first and foremost. But I'm just a grammarian, and so its hypocrisy does.

They've learned your lessons.

(Ah, again I ask, I ask myself, and not without anxiety, whether your idea of the homeland has become so just, so fair that it's worth a man's life, or ten years of a man's life, or ten days of a man's life.)

WHEREIN IS ESSAYED AN EXPLANATION OF HYPOCRISY, FALSEHOOD, LYING, AND SCORN

I must not have expressed myself clearly. M. Claude Morgan, answering in the *Lettres,* assures me that he loves his homeland, that he adores it, that he's a super-patriot, and that others are terrible

20. *Les Lettres Françaises,* 18 April 1947.

antipatriots. I never doubted it. I mean that I never doubted his answer. Because this is 1947. In 1940 he would have told me, with Thorez, that a communist doesn't have a homeland. In 1935, with Aragon, that France is the vermin of the world. Fine. But as for the question I posed, not one word. I seem to have handled it badly, I lack the knack for discussions that slide through politics. I'll try again.

Take a country split between Reds and Whites. For a while the Direction of Things is rather whitish. Then comes a day when the Reds declare: "You took us this far, and that's far enough. Let the war come. We won't defend the country unless it turns red." The Whites are naturally annoyed. They mutter something like: ". . . a dozen bullets in the flesh."

Fine. In a few years power passes, if not to the Reds, then to the Pinks. Now it's time for the Whites to start saying: "Look at what you've done to the country! This mud, this mess! If war comes, don't count on us.—Disgusting, say the Reds. Look at those people who've stuffed our minds with their homeland! A homeland for their mutual funds, their portfolios, their trusts, yes . . ."

Two great leaders desert.

Then a war really does come, and no one can say that the Reds, or for that matter the Whites, do it with any brilliance. The great leader of the Reds begins by deserting (to a foreign country). The great leader of the Whites does pretty much the same (to the interior); and there he gains, with our enemy's help, an opportunity to massacre more than a few Reds.

But the country finds itself liberated (with the help of some foreign armies). The Reds are returned to power, and it's time to exterminate a few Whites. No problem for them: they have the power. Ah, but that's not enough, they also want the right. What right? The laws, they say, are clear . . .—Let's talk about them. Those are the same laws that have been crushing you for the past five years.—Those Whites betrayed the homeland!—Given the chance, you would have agreed to betray it too. So tell the truth. You exterminate them for being Whites.

There's always a time to renounce allegory and put our cards on the table. So perhaps I can speak directly about Henri Béraud. I feel no sympathy or admiration for the man. I don't seek to minimize his faults: it's entirely true that he was abusive toward Gide around 1920, and toward England after 1930. He showed a stupid admiration for the Marshall, and called M. Muselier a "laundry-boat admiral," which was an unfair, vulgar thing to do. Granted all this, why on earth did you condemn him to death? The one you struck down, was he not a former communist (or communiser), a member of Arac who became a pamphleteer for *Gringoire* and Salengro's persecutor—in short, a renegade?

Yes indeed, and Charles Maurras—himself a good writer and doubtless a great one, who never stopped denouncing the warlike projects of our enemy (at about the same time you invited France to disarm)—and proposed in 1918 a regime (which you only now decide should apply to Germany)? Did his clairvoyance call for death, or for life imprisonment? Out of the ten thousand pages he was able to write under Vichy, I know that you managed to find two lines resembling an informer's. Is this the reason, or do you blame him instead for his bodyguards, his threats, his endless plots?

—What, then the Republic would have no right to defend itself?—Ah, very good! Then say so! I'm not concerned with politics here, what bothers me is your hypocrisy. I'm afraid I see it completely controlling your Purge, justifying its caprice and its tortures: a shameless farrago of justice and vengeance, decent people who were deceived thrown into the same bag with scum, special juries spitting in the face of the accused, all those partisan hatreds vaporizing the unity of France.

I simply say in passing what everyone sees. I'm not assuming anything you wouldn't recognize. Julian Benda "would have regarded collaboration," says he, "as a gift from the gods, had Germany only supplied a regime superior to our own."[21] So why do you blame those other collaborators, Benda, whose massacre you demand? For having betrayed their homeland? No; since you yourself were ready to betray it. In effect, for admiring a regime that makes you vomit. For belonging to a party not your own. You're not a patriot, and if, in one situation or another, you happened to find the homeland on your side, you can say in all loyalty that the fault is not your own.[22] You're a partisan, something entirely dif-

21. Julien Teppe, *Enquête sur le Nationalisme,* p. 6.
22. Cf. J. Benda: "Oui, je suis nationaliste, mais ce n'est pas ma faute" (*L'Ordre,* 25 June 1946).

ferent. Words have a precise meaning that we ought to respect. A taste for moral values, faith in justice, love for the people, all are laudable feelings; but none is called patriotism. Any more than exoticism, or the pleasures of anthropophagy. But what, then, is patriotism?

Patriotism, what is it?

Well, France is an impetus [*élan*], extending from the Revolution of '89 (and from long before '89) to the revolt of the Maquis. It's also a land of hills and plains tracing their little path from the Rhine to the Pyrenees. Now, patriotism consists in not separating this bodily France from the spiritual France, any more than a man's face is separated from his profile. It's a love for the homeland; it's also the firm will to make it better. It's still more: it's deciding to refuse benefits coming from places other than France (just as a child learns to refuse gifts from a stranger). And I won't deny this involves a strange, even a paradoxical feeling. But love has its mysteries: everyone knows a mother loves her children, and yet she never quits—at the price of a thousand vexations and hassles—until she has made them, as she puts it, better. If she chooses to put them in a Public Assistance program in order to adopt others she prefers, then perhaps I'd say she shows a taste for intelligence or virtue. I would never say, no, not for anything in the world would I say that she demonstrates a great maternal love. Nor Benda, a vital patriotism.

This is what I've been getting at: since no one has yet decreed the existence of guilty opinions calling for death, the pacifists of 1914 have no right to appear so aggressive toward the pacifists of 1940. Nor those executed in 1915 (if I may put it so) the right to scorn those executed in 1945. From the standpoint of the homeland itself, each is the other's peer: it's the difference between "the following day" and "the day following."

This being said, shouldn't some opinions be considered criminal? It's an interesting question. At least have the courage to pose it. State your opinions frankly: imperialist France in 1870 didn't deserve the love of Rimbaud; or reactionary France in 1914 the confidence of Rolland; or bourgeois France in 1930 the loyalty of Aragon. Or radical France in 1939 . . . "We've changed," they say.

You think you've changed, fine. But the ones you accuse, perhaps they've changed too. Did you bother to ask them before putting them on your blacklist? And I also see, cited on that list, more than one who willingly fought, more than one soldier who was wounded. Why not, if your recent ardor is so sincere, at least let them benefit from a preferential obscurity? I see, for example, the name of Armand Petitjean; head of a free unit starting in '39, cited in '40, returning from the war with one hand intact, his left hand. He still fights, starting in '43, in the battles of the Liberation, and recruits, at the request of a new prefect, a thousand boys with guns to fight in the streets of Paris. He then returns to the front with his left hand, leading a Moroccan *goum*; cited, at the end of '44, in the Vosges; and in early '45, in Germany. He's a hero, someone I envy. Yet you place him, for twelve mischievous articles he wrote under Vichy, not on your roll of honor, but on your list of infamy.

That workers of the eleventh hour should be feted before anyone else, this I accept. They're also the ones about whom we'd begun to despair. But when they themselves start jailing or strangling the workers—call them, if you prefer, the slaves—of the ten hours preceding, then all can see that they exaggerate. All start to wonder why they exaggerate.

The patriot is modest.

Why, then, do you exaggerate? A sincere patriot seems more calm. More modest. (He knows that patriotism isn't so easy.) He doesn't try at any price to convert the antipatriots of centuries gone by. He readily admits that Rimbaud was as disgusted with his country as he was with his mother. When Romain Rolland says that the cause of France in '14 was a crime against humanity, the patriot doesn't conclude that Rolland never separated the cause of humanity from the cause of France. When Martin-Chauffier says: "we don't judge," the patriot wouldn't have it said to Martin-Chauffier: "It's the homeland that judges. It condemns you to death." When Jean Cassou says: "What nice weather!", a patriot wouldn't have it said to Jean Cassou: "This weather is actually French!" In short, he doesn't resort to tricks, and if he finds himself referring to the homeland as a bleeding fetish, he doesn't claim that he means the homeland of others—of trusts and portfolios—rather than his own, the real homeland. All these lies would strike him as sordid.

But sordid isn't saying much. That you lie at all is what matters.

That a fascist would lie isn't very important. It's possible he'd lie from conviction. Because he considers—this is indeed what makes him a fascist—that the people have no right to the truth, that they couldn't endure it, that it would go to their head. And so he lies, if I may say so, faithfully. When Maurras argues tenaciously that Dreyfus is guilty, he only means that it would be desirable and decent, that it would be best for the whole world, if Dreyfus were guilty. That Dreyfus, if he were truly a patriot, would agree to be guilty. (We've known a few trials where Dreyfus agreed to be convinced.) Fine. But the democrat, for his part, begins by agreeing that people have a right to the truth, just as they have a right to happiness—and that the two can even be the same, that lying and unhappiness are a pair. And so the lying democrat begins by lying to himself. He tells two lies. He betrays the truth. That's the least of it: he betrays both his principles and his raison d'être. He testifies against democracy. He degrades himself and the rest of us. It follows, then, that his reason for lying would be a thousand times more serious than the fascist's. But what could that reason be? And what, finally, were you trying to hide?

Here you'll accuse me of kicking at doors already opened. Claude Morgan is so surprised at the sincerity of my suspicions that he calls me a "false ingénue." I don't mind the false ingénue. This, finally, is what I heard from all sides, and had trouble accepting: you, like Benda, would be ready to receive, with open arms, an enemy that would impress upon you the regime of your dreams. Were it not for an accident of history—a war declared against Russia rather than its ally, Germany—you would, all of you, be collaborators, and Brasillach or Rebatet the heroes of the Resistance. In short, you were good citizens of France by chance, and members of the Resistance by accident.

I know the conjecture is serious. You fail to see that your lies and tricks end up making it forceful and true. Don't call yourselves patriots. I find you completely committed to proving you are. But your proofs are false; your evidence, tainted.

What to say about your blacklist now? We've always had, in our literature, a few amateur police: Restif, Murger, Casanova (the writer, not the Director). We weren't otherwise proud of them. Ah, it's also known that the heat of battle, or a sacred love for the Homeland, can justify, can even ennoble, an accuser. But what's an accuser without faith, an accuser without patriotism? Lower than the lowest of the dregs.

NOR IS THE HOMELAND A SPECIALTY

Our homeland was saved several years ago. It was saved by men who weren't greatly burdened by the homeland, who didn't always put France at the forefront of their concerns—who often put a foreign power foremost. Who went to war as if on a whaling expedition or a tiger shoot: with a lively desire to get it over with, fierce, filled with the joy of living abroad and in ambush, hard to advise, hard to lead. They never mentioned the homeland. They themselves were the homeland. It's entirely different; until now, we haven't seen so clearly just how it's entirely different.

For it happened, conversely, that the French whose homeland was their daily bread and, as it were, their specialty—great politicians, professors, industrialists, important people in all walks of life, alas!, and even those of the young who wanted to judge all things in terms of France alone—well, the least to be said is that none was very brilliant. (Except in various arguments and demonstrations, trying to justify the armistice, and the ruin of the country they pretended to serve. And then they suddenly shone far brighter than necessary.) What a strange adventure: France was almost ruined by men who prayed every day to the goddess France; it was saved by (among others) men who tossed the French army every day into the waste basket. In sum, it's as if it were dangerous to talk too much about the homeland, unwise to see it face to face. There exists, therefore, a mystery of the homeland, like the mysteries of language and Letters. Who knows, a neighboring mystery, no doubt. Because confusing the bodily homeland with the spiritual homeland, in order to recognize only *one* homeland, may not be so different from confusing words with ideas. It's the very same absurdity. White writers, you'll never worry enough about becom-

Where everything happens upside down.

ing specialists in the Homeland—and if its defense has won you any privileges, I would, if I were you, renounce them.

You will ask me: "What would be left of the Céné if we took away its blacklist?" Ah! for subjects, you'll find all you need. But here's one I'd like to propose right away: prove me a liar in turn. Decide to remain true, in the future, to your past. Swear once and for all—whatever foreigner tries to control the homeland from abroad; coming someday, who knows? to occupy France perhaps, summoned (like Germany) by more than one Frenchman—swear to oppose it with the same tenacity and resistance that united us shortly ago. Prepare for that fight from this day onward. Feeble and meager as my assistance may be, I'll be proud to stand at your side.

Little tasks of defense and illustration.

After this, I'd gladly propose to you those little exercises of defense and illustration just discussed. And you might find them trivial, even frivolous. No doubt. But they can soon lead, as you saw, to more serious issues. (As in tales and myths, a word well pronounced allows joy to rush in; a little lie sends hope flying away.) Serious issues indeed, and hard to the extent that they can't be seen face to face, approachable only through chance, obliquely—through the chance, precisely, of *joquets* and *métingues*, languages, games, and literature.

Perhaps, on the other hand, someone will say that this is just a lot of pride and confusion, and that the situation of France (and French) in today's world hardly justifies such concern. But no, I hope no one says this. It's as if someone just told us he isn't yet rich enough to be honest. We know ahead of time what happens next: no one's ever rich enough.

Praise for foreign words.

Ah! Someone adds that there are more urgent problems, among them "W.W. trie." (I definitely prefer to call it "W.W. trie," Petitjean's right. "World-wide three" is too familiar, as if it were already here. In point of fact, "jockey" may mean that we no longer bet at the racetrack; and "meeting," that we stay quietly at home, reflecting on politics. Well, if foreign words mean not getting involved with something that you've firmly decided to leave foreign, then long live foreign words! But I'd like to be a little more certain about this.) As for the "W.W.," you can sleep, good people, in peace. If it's ever unleashed, it won't be your fault. There's no hope that you'll play the principal part. It'll fly over your head. Lucky if it just flies. And even with atom bombs and the like, no one can say you're in the avant-garde of progress. Try to resign yourself, hard as that may be: history, for the moment, leaves you in peace. Perhaps this wouldn't be a bad time to study—but if so, then in depth, minutely, with rage, giving it everything, and cleaning, to start with, and thoroughly, too, your instruments as well as your words—things that you know about.

These, in sum, are the most serious. We're a little tired of man's fate. Myself—seeing how things happen—I rather get the idea that we don't belong to that fate; that it must have been played a little too fast, with a bad roll of the dice; that we ought to get back to the start. And no more cheating with words, any more than with men.

That's all I had to say, finally. *Salut et Fraternité.*

APPENDIX: THREE NOTES ON THE HOMELAND

Too often, I'm afraid, the question in the three following notes will be about me. Because we reach the truth (or stay there) as best we can. Pleasure at being right, aggravation at an undeserved reproach, even wounded vanity are ways as good as any, provided we move beyond them.

At issue here, in effect, is a particularly difficult truth: the truth involving the homeland. We can take the measure of its difficulty by reflecting that good French, believing that they loyally served France, find themselves scolded as traitors every day by other French, who loudly brag about being patriots, all the time knowing very well that they aren't.

But do we have to be patriotic? Ah, that's a question I didn't ask. And we no doubt attach a high price to the accident of being born Chinese, Czech, or French if we grant it the slightest political value. It's also a way of exposing ourselves to various dangers. Dangers, moreover, that we've recognized. I'll get back to these.

I.
Romain Rolland; or, Reasons for Lying

In the first answer it gave me, the Executive Committee of the Céné wrote:

> ALTHOUGH HE ADMITTED THE LEVITY OF HIS REMARKS, JEAN PAULHAN DOESN'T DEFEND THEM ANY THE LESS . . .[1]

Now I never said my remarks were light. I said they were "simplistic and summary, as a conversation is apt to be."[2] (I was actually referring to an interview.) And I promptly added that they were perfectly correct. But here's something more serious:

> IN DISMISSING ROLLAND ALONG WITH THE COLLABORATORS FROM 1940 TO 1944, PAULHAN PROVIDES AN ARGUMENT FOR THOSE DEFENDING A PETAIN OR A DARNAND BECAUSE OF THEIR CONDUCT DURING THE WAR OF 1914.

And further on:

> PAULHAN HAS ADVANCED THE IDEA . . . THAT ROMAIN ROLLAND IN 1914–1918 BEHAVED LIKE CHÂTEAUBRIANT IN 1940–1944.[3]

---

1. *Les Lettres Françaises,* 14 February 1947.
2. *Le Littéraire,* 1 February 1947.
3. *Les Lettres Françaises,* 21 March 1947.

This is false. I advanced no such thing. I "advanced" the very opposite. I began by saying that from 1940 to 1944 Châteaubriant committed treason—that he was *precisely* a traitor (line 102). I added later that Rolland, like Châteaubriant in the war of '40 (before the armistice, in other words), *betrayed the cause* of France during the war of '14 (line 154).

So yes, this accusation is a lie, plain and simple. Curious, though, that someone might commit it (with all its evident crudeness). Curious that it could pass, could seem plausible even for a moment, that its stupidity wouldn't leap instantly into view. In the end, it could prove to be a highly instructive lie.

I recall the facts. With his scorn for our democracy, with the infinite admiration he swears for Hitler, Châteaubriant betrays, after 1936—more seriously after 1939—the *cause* of France. He doesn't *betray* France, properly speaking, until the day he does business with the conquering enemy and founds, with their support, a newspaper in the occupied zone.

But Rolland, for his part, resides in Switzerland, where he tells us, writes us, lets us know in a thousand ways why our own French cause wasn't worth any more than the cause of the other side—maybe less. Is this to betray France? Is it the same as doing business with the enemy? No. It's very simply betraying the cause of France. Do you doubt this for an instant? If so, then imagine Châteaubriant publishing his own *Above the Battle* in Geneva during the war: tossing Hitler into the sack with Daladier, Churchill with Goering. What to say? What not to say? Certainly that "betraying the cause" would have seemed a thousand times too weak. Why the lie, then, and what trumped-up quarrel are they trying to pick with me?

And yet this gives rise, it must be said, to a baffling puzzle.

*
* *

Note that this puzzle can't come from the men involved. Rolland and Châteaubriant belong to those writers putting their soul on the line at all times: warm and noble, rather grandiloquent. Personal, and tending to heresy: the first drawing on theosophy, the second on hermeticism. (Might I add: with a confused mind.) Both, too, cherishing the Germanic soul. Fraternal friends, furthermore, each holding the other in the highest regard. Divided, however, by a political abyss: the one oscillating between anarchy and communism; the other, between an integral monarchy and a sacral state. Châteaubriant, the Rolland of the right; Rolland, the Châteaubriant of the left. The parallel is unavoidable.

If the puzzle doesn't come from the men, does it come, perhaps, from their situations?

Here I find a curious hint in the open letter that Madame Romain Rolland addressed to me:

> I THINK IT HELPS TO POINT OUT THAT THE VERY PERSONS FULL OF HATRED AND BAD FAITH WHO ACCUSED ROMAIN ROLLAND IN 1914, ARE THE SAME WHO WELCOMED, JOYFULLY FOR THE MOST PART, THE GERMAN VICTORY IN 1940, AND WHO SERVED THE ENEMY WITH ZEAL.[4]

Yes, that's roughly the case. Just as more than a few republicans could be found celebrating the Empire's defeats in 1870, so more than one reactionary was found, in 1940, celebrating the ruin of the Republic—serving our enemy with zeal. Barrès, a conservative himself, foresaw this singular attitude as early as 1903. The reasons he evokes are exactly those of Châteaubriant:

> IT'S THE CONSERVATIVES WHO WILL ACCEPT, WHO WILL SUMMON FOREIGNERS. YES: TODAY'S PATRIOTS, PROUD MEN SICK OF A SHRUNKEN FRANCE AND A LIFE OF HUMILIATION, WILL SUMMON A REGIME, A FOREIGN INTERVENTION, FINALLY GRANTING THEM THE JOY OF PARTICIPATING IN A GREAT COLLECTIVE LIFE—AND WE SHALL FIND, ON THE OPPOSITE SIDE, A RESISTANCE TO FOREIGNERS PERSONIFIED BY PACIFIST DEMAGOGUERY.[5]

As to whether every reactionary is "full of hatred and bad faith," that's a different question. Perhaps Madame Romain Rolland answers a little too quickly.

Let's proceed. The letter continues:

> ... WE COULD DEDUCE FROM YOUR EXPRESSION: "CHATEAUBRIANT, HIS FRIEND AND DISCIPLE," THAT EVERY FRIEND AND DISCIPLE OF ROMAIN ROLLAND WAS SUSPECTED OF TREASON. BUT YOU KNOW PERFECTLY WELL THAT MOST OF THEM EITHER SERVED WITH DISTINCTION OR DIED IN THE RESISTANCE.[6]

In fact I know this very well. Yes, more than one of Rolland's pacifist friends displayed joyful courage during the Resistance. (And I'd promptly add that many of Rolland's disciples, in the war of 1914, showed all the more courage given their despair.) But what does this prove, and what are we arguing over?

Over what do we argue? Ah! Without ever admitting it directly, you let me know in a hundred ways. Thus the Committee of the Céné:

> IN DISMISSING ROLLAND ALONG WITH THE COLLABORATORS OF 1940 TO 1944 ...

---

4. *Le Littéraire,* 1 February 1947.
5. *Cahiers,* vol. III, p. 265.
6. *Le Littéraire,* 1 February 1947.

(That's the lie I mentioned. Let us proceed.)

> ... PAULHAN TRIES TO ESTABLISH A SIMILARITY BETWEEN THE TWO WARS.[7]

(But no! I don't try to establish it. I acknowledge it.)

So Marc Beigbeder:

> IN 1940, THE GOOD GERMANY DIED, A FURUNCLE KILLED IT, CONSUMING ITS ENTIRE BODY AND SOUL . . . IN 1914, THE GOOD GERMANY WAS STILL LIVING, CAPABLE OF RESPONDING, OF RETURNING . . .[8]

(Perhaps. But we deal with events, not intentions. I simply observe that it never did return, never made that response.)

So Edith Thomas:

> DESPITE JEAN PAULHAN'S ASSERTION THAT THE WAR OF 1914 AND THE WAR OF 1940–1944 ARE MERELY ONE AND THE SAME WAR (THIRTY YEARS LONG), IT WOULD BE WELL TO RECALL SOME ELEMENTARY TRUTHS; PEACE ISN'T WAR, THE WEIMAR REPUBLIC WASN'T HITLER'S REGIME . . .[9]

(But no. I don't assert, I report. It was one and the same war, with, of course, a long interval of peace. The hundred years' war had a few of its own.)

So Martin-Chauffier:

> IN 1914, THE "“CAUSE OF FRANCE" WAS NOT PERHAPS ENTIRELY THE SAME AS IN '40. WITHOUT FORCING A DISTINCTION, OBVIOUS IN ANY EVENT, BETWEEN THE TWO WARS . . .[10]

Maybe I'm naive. For me, it's mainly the similarities that leap into view. Because then as now, after all, we were attacked; then as now, by an enemy sure of itself, confident of its race, and imbued with its own superiority. And we, doubting ourselves, were ill-prepared to defend, ill-prepared even to think about war. Then as now, the French had to defend the land of their parents and children; they did this, sometimes well, sometimes badly; with an almost unanimous enthusiasm in 1914, in 1939 with an indifference greatly aggravated by communist obstruction and reactionary mistrust. But finally, winners or losers, in civil or in military uniform, we were facing the same enemy. Nor had the stakes of the combat changed. Above all, don't tell me that a police state, tortures, and concentration

---

7. *Les Lettres Françaises,* 14 February 1947.
8. *Esprit,* 1947, p. 608.
9. *La Marseillaise,* 18 February 1947.
10. *Les Lettres Françaises,* 22 January 1947.

camps are anything new: Russia has its own, and Romain Rolland denounced them starting in 1922.[11]

What quarrel are they trying to pick with me? I can see it very well. I'm not as dumb as I look. You want to me to know that in 1914 it was brave, and perhaps even right, to betray the cause of a bourgeois and capitalist France allied to czarist Russia, and that in 1941 it was ignoble to betray the cause of a France allied to the Soviets, and tomorrow perhaps, who knows? turning soviet itself. And that Romain Rolland's error, serious as it may have been, followed the trend of history—precisely a democratic or communist trend, while the error of Châteaubriant went the other way. Finally, that the war of '14 was a war for the right, and that the war of '41 was a war for the left.

And I would certainly want this conviction to be deep, even passionate. I can also see that it explains your lie—without justifying it. For if wars among nations, for you, are only civil wars, then betraying the cause of one's homeland, and betraying the homeland itself, are all one and the same thing (since homelands are only causes); and you almost don't play tricks when describing my views as you do. But if that's how you really feel, then say so frankly, without all those ruses or allusions. Above all, don't talk the homeland to death. Because, finally, you don't care about that homeland. Because you've agreed to argue, anyway, as if there were no room for the homeland.

II.
Julien Benda; Or, A Confusion of Ideas

M. Julien Benda is so happy with his article *The Paulhan Case* that he reprinted it in *Lettres* after publishing it in *Ordre.*[12] Not that this is something to be proud of. But you be the judge:

---

11. Cf.: "It is unhappily too certain that, for most of the ruling minds of the Russian Revolution . . . all is subordinated to reason of state.
"I don't combat one reason of state in order to serve another. And militarism, police terror or brutal force aren't sanctified for me by being the instrument of a communist dictatorship . . ." (Romain Rolland, "*Lettre à Barbusse,*" *l'Art libre,* January 1922).

12. 27 October 1947.

> THE PLACE THAT JEAN PAULHAN GAVE TO A FLATTERER OF NAZISM IN HIS *Cahiers de la Pléiade* HAS OUTRAGED THE WIDOW OF THE LATE LAMENTED GROETHUYSEN, DISGUSTED AT SEEING HIS NAME CONFUSED WITH APOLOGISTS FOR HIS ASSASSINS. I'M TOLD THAT THE FORMER DIRECTOR OF THE *Nouvelle Revue Française* DEFENDS HIMSELF BY ANSWERING THAT . . .

(Here Benda cites and refutes various arguments I supposedly made. He concludes:)

> IS THERE BAD FAITH IN PAULHAN? A WEAKNESS OF MIND? A CLOWN'S HUMOR? A PSYCHOLOGICAL PROBLEM? WHY NOT ALL THREE?

An odd procedure. "They assure me . . ." says Benda. Why didn't he assure himself? My "defense" appears on page 269 of the very *Cahiers* he vituperates. Is that a place (as he says) to find laziness, senility, or bad faith? In truth M. Julien Benda, who has never hesitated to exterminate his colleagues, has yet to resign himself to reading them. But he doesn't usually admit this.

One other word. Bernard Groethuysen, whose name I regret to see mixed up in this quarrel, died last year of lung cancer. He was never tortured, not even bothered by our enemies. He had no "assassins." M. Benda, who knew Groethuysen very well, is aware of this fact. Here I see only a lie, or senility.

But I move on to the arguments.

*
* *

> THEY ASSURE ME . . .

Benda then writes,

> . . . THAT PAULHAN'S DEFENSE CONSISTS IN CLAIMING THAT LITERATURE IS SO IMPORTANT THAT IT TAKES PRECEDENCE OVER ANY MORAL PRINCIPLE, LIKE PATRIOTISM, OR ANY OTHER . . .

I said nothing of the sort. I think nothing of the sort. M. Benda, who was poorly assured, continues:

> I CERTAINLY ADMIT THAT WE MIGHT PRAISE THE WRITINGS OF A TRAITOR LIKE BRASILLACH WHEN WE FIND THEM BEAUTIFUL (WHICH IS NOT THE CASE FOR ME), EVEN THOUGH WE EXECUTED HIM FOR TREASON. LIKEWISE THE ENGLISH, WHO CONSIDERED OSCAR WILDE AS ONE OF THEIR GREAT WRITERS, JAILED HIM FOR HIS OUTRAGE AGAINST MORALS. I WAS ASTONISHED THE OTHER DAY BY THE ATTITUDE OF M. EMILE HENRIOT TOWARD M. EMMANUEL

> BERL . . . OUR EMINENT COLLEAGUE AT *Le Monde* WRITES ME THAT HE RECOGNIZES A JUST IDEA WHEN HE SEES ONE, AND THAT HE THOUGHT HE FOUND ONE IN A RECENT BOOK BY M. BERL. FINE. I ONLY WISH THAT, IN PRAISING M. BERL'S WISE VIEWS, HE HAD ALSO CONDEMNED, WITH AT LEAST ONE LITTLE WORD, HIS VIOLENT MUNICHISM IN 1938. WE ARE A PEOPLE OF DISTINCT IDEAS.

Quite right! And who shall decide if a text is beautiful? Here we should summon the critics, I suppose (not the magistrates). Who shall decide if a man is guilty? The judges, I suppose (not the literary critics).

In fact, this was the whole point of my little petition in support of authors being prevented from writing. Is this to set too great a value on literature? No, it's leaving it in its place, and the judges in theirs. It enlarges the distinction of ideas into a division of functions. I'm convinced that M. Benda, had he thought about it for a while, would hold to no other view. If M. Berl did a disservice to the interests of France, let Justice send him to jail. If he wrote a good and honest page, let criticism show its gratitude. In a word, by commenting on Berl's text, M. Henriot was only doing his job. And in replying with a reference to M. Berl's Munichism (which has nothing to do with the matter), M. Benda failed to do his own. Henriot distinguishes, Benda confuses. Elsewhere, however, he writes:

> THE FORMER VIZIER OF THE N.R.F. DECLARED SHORTLY AGO THAT A GROUP OF WRITERS,

(myself, without vanity)

> RATHER THAN REJECTING ITS WRONG-HEADED MEMBERS, OUGHT INSTEAD TO EXAMINE THEIR ERRORS AND REFUTE THEM, ASKING IF THEY CONTAIN A KERNEL OF TRUTH—IN SHORT, RECOGNIZING FROM THE START A CERTAIN *right to error* ON THE AUTHOR'S BEHALF (WHO PUTS HIS SOUL IN DANGER, AND SUFFERS A HUNDRED HAZARDS ON OUR BEHALF). PHYSICISTS DO THE SAME. AND TO SOME DEGREE EACH OF US IS ALSO A PHYSICIST.
>
> THE READER HAS ALREADY JUDGED THIS THINKER WHO ASSIGNS THE NAME OF ERROR TO THE ACT OF BETRAYING ONE'S COUNTRY. THE READER WONDERS WHAT A PHYSICIST'S EXPERIMENT COULD HAVE IN COMMON WITH SOMEONE SCREAMING AT US EVERY DAY TO BEAT UP OUR COUNTRY IN EVERY POSSIBLE WAY; OR AGAIN, IF WE WERE TRYING, LIKE A CHARLES BENOIST OR AN ETIENNE LAMY—WITHOUT THREATS OR DIRECT ACTION—TO DETERMINE SCIENTIFICALLY WHETHER ONE REGIME IS BETTER THAN ANOTHER, THE READER WONDERS WHY THIS MERELY IDEOLOGICAL ATTITUDE (WHICH MIGHT IN ALL RIGOR BE CALLED AN EXPERIMENT) MIGHT BE "DANGEROUS," AND WHY ALL OF US SHOULDN'T ADOPT IT. THE

READER IS NOT A LITTLE SURPRISED TO LEARN THAT MAURRAS, WHO PRIDED HIMSELF ON KNOWING THE FACTS AND SCORNING ALL MORALITY, "PUT HIS SOUL INTO PLAY," THOUGH WE MIGHT FIND SOMETHING OF THE SORT AT WORK IN PEOPLE LIKE RENAN OR LAMENNAIS, WHO COMMITTED THEIR ENTIRE BEING TO A DRAMA OF CONSCIENCE.[13]

Here again, let's distinguish. There's room to differentiate, with Maurras, between two pathways, and one is purely intellectual: it consists in establishing (or in trying to establish), through observation, experience, and law, that one regime—a monarchy, in fact—is better than another. In *The Future of Intelligence,* as in *Inquiry* or *The Road to Paradise,* Maurras proceeds very much like a Renan or a Lamy. His conclusions, like his method—a guiding empiricism—refer to the logic of proof, and if he finally decides "only to know the facts" (which of course is not entirely the case), he does so at the end of a long chain of reflections which, in themselves, are far from being pure and simple facts. But once the doctrine has been fixed, Maurras pursues—particularly with the Action Française—a second pathway, purely practical and pragmatic: his only aim—and he admits this—is to beat down democracy at every possible turn. Fine. Between the two pathways, I see more or less the same difference as between learning how to split atoms and detonating the bomb on Bikini. I can willingly agree with you, Benda, that the political and conspiratorial Maurras belongs in the courts of law; and now you can agree that Maurras the researcher and natural philosopher pertains to our own examination. You know this better than anyone, having written one of the finest critiques of integral nationalism that I know of.

Someone will ask me: if we follow you, shouldn't Maurras have published his findings?—But of course! Certainly he should have published his findings, and, if they were so received, should have accepted their condemnation. Ought, in brief, to have risked his body after risking his soul. That's how his research, his reflection—or, if you prefer, his experiments—were "dangerous." (But I'm ashamed to spell out such obvious points.)

Here, as I only too well know, you'll tell me too that very few writers could really be said to run intellectual risks on our behalf, or pursue the truth through blood and tears. But of course! Did I say otherwise? No doubt there are very few indeed. But those are the only ones I discuss. Those are the ones I care about.

Might I add: the only ones you should care about. And why should we worry about the mob from the press or radio? A Ferdonnet, a Laubreaux? I've never written, I believe, on the side of a Laubreaux, and I don't plan

13. *Fontaine,* March 1947.

to start tomorrow. I merely reproach the Céné for confusing, on its blacklist, the Ferdonnets with a Montherlant, or the Laubreaux with a Céline.

However, Julien Benda concludes:

> THE SAME DOCTOR MAINTAINS, FINALLY, THAT THE DRIEUS AND THEIR COLLEAGUES WERE ONLY TRYING TO ACTUALIZE THE THESIS OF MY "DISCOURSE TO THE EUROPEAN NATION," AND THAT, IN CONDEMNING THEM, I SHOW THE INCOHERENCE OF MY OWN IDEAS. AS IF THERE WERE ANY EQUIVALENCE BETWEEN, ON THE ONE HAND, INVITING MY FELLOW CITIZENS TO ABANDON THEIR NATIONALISM FOR AN INSTITUTION TRANSCENDING NATIONALISM, AND, ON THE OTHER HAND, SURRENDERING TO A FANATICALLY NATIONALIST NATION THAT INTENDS, IN THE NAME OF THE "CHOSEN RACE," TO ENSLAVE THEM. SOON WE'LL BE HEARING THAT THESE TRAITORS ACTED LIKE STUDENTS OF MALEBRANCHE OR FENELON . . .

No, I never said anything of the sort. I could even swear that it never occurred to me to connect Benda with Malebranche. I asked the following question: were we men of the left—on the good side for once!—justified in so violently reproaching men of the right for being alienated from the homeland, when we never stopped showing them how? That's the question I posed. I pose it still, and suppose it's embarrassing, since Benda needs so many errors or tricks to deflect it. So who is he mad at, and what does he find so upsetting?

What upsets him I see very well. I don't want to flatter M. Benda, and I won't go so far as to claim that he invented Hitler. But he must have created, unless we read him very poorly, more than one Hitlerian. For the entire thesis of the *Discourse* argues that we have to renounce France in order to create Europe. And how to create Europe? First, says Benda, by "glorifying certain heroes of History."[14] Which ones? Ah, precisely those who wanted Europe. Certainly not a Louis XIV, or a Louis XI, "entirely concerned with consolidating their territory,"[15] but rather "a Barbarossa, a Frederic of Sicily, Charles the Fifth, above all Napoleon."[16]

It's only too natural to add Hitler to the list. "Had the Hohenstaufens," Benda says again, "been able to unite Germany and Italy, the world would have enjoyed a beautiful peace for centuries on end." We think we're listening to Goebbels.

Understand us. Benda's thesis isn't absurd. It could well be the case, if our nationalisms are to be abolished, that Europe will require the preliminary triumph of *one* nationalism to accomplish that goal. Thus the vic-

14. *Discours à la Nation Européenne,* pp. 49 ff.
15. p. 49.
16. p. 49.

tory of *one* class—the proletariat—ought to lead, according to the Marxists, to a classless society. But Benda, in 1936, never saw Hitler coming. "Never again will we see," he writes (sadly), "a man who decides to conquer Europe in order to unite it."

Well, we saw him again, but Benda—why, I really don't know—was never ready to recognize him. Every historian has his weaknesses, and I don't begrudge Benda his own. I only believe that he'd never confuse, and so obstinately, the function of a judge with that of a critic, or an intellectual error with a criminal act, or the "equivalence" of two theses with their causal relation, if he weren't already committed to denying his own responsibility and to concealing the incoherence to which his thought was driven by his refusal of patriotism.

III.
Claude Morgan; Or, Manipulated Incoherence

Claude Morgan, they assure me, also answered me. He himself seems sure of this. And so I shall cite him:

> PAULHAN FORCES US TO TAKE HIM SERIOUSLY, FOR HE FEELS A NEED TO ENTRUST HIS LATEST EPISTLE TO THE WEEKLY *Carrefour*, WHICH, THOUGH JEAN PAULHAN DENIES THAT HE'S POLITICAL, GIVES HIS INTERVENTION A VERY PRECISE POLITICAL MEANING. I CERTAINLY DON'T INTEND TO ANSWER FOR THE C.N.E. HE ATTACKS, BEING NO BETTER QUALIFIED THAN ANYONE ELSE TO DO SO. BUT JEAN PAULHAN'S ATTACK IS ALSO DIRECTED AGAINST THE *Lettres Françaises*, THOSE *Lettres Françaises* TO WHICH HE WAS RECENTLY SO ATTACHED THAT HE ASKED ME, ON THE DAY AFTER THE LIBERATION, TO MENTION ON THE MASTHEAD THAT HE WAS ONE OF ITS FOUNDERS, SOMETHING NOT ENTIRELY TRUE, SINCE THE PAPER'S FIRST FIVE NUMBERS APPEARED WITHOUT HIM. AND SO THE *Lettres Françaises* REPLIES TO JEAN PAULHAN . . .[17]

Here we find a lot of mistakes in the space of a few words. I entrusted my letter, not to *Carrefour*, but to the *Nouvelles Epîtres* of Vercors, Bernanos, and Martin-Chauffier. *Carrefour* was restricted to a reprint ten days after. That's the first point.

---

17. *Les Lettres Françaises*, 1 August 1947.

A second point: during the liberation, the *Lettres Françaises* graciously chose to allot me fifty shares as a founder—at a thousand francs per share, if you please. The announcement itself was made at the first public meeting of the Céné. I for my part was rather embarrassed by these capitalist gestures. The time came to ask Claude Morgan: "Won't you just call me a founder? That would be just fine." As indeed it was. But Claude Morgan's sense of humor is as weak as his sense of the truth.

On his last point, I limit myself to citing the brief *History of the "Lettres Françaises,"* which appeared in the paper's first issue (9 September 1944), under the signatures of Jacques Debû-Bridel and Claude Morgan:

> . . . ON THE ADVICE OF JEAN PAULHAN, JACQUES DECOUR AND I DECIDED IT WAS NECESSARY TO PUT A WEEKLY INTO CIRCULATION . . .

Further on:

> THE LITTLE TEAM FOR THE DEBUT, WHICH WE INITIALLY FORMED AROUND JEAN PAULHAN IN JEAN BLANZAT'S APARTMENT, INCLUDED VILDRAC, GUEHENNO, JEAN VAUDAL, MAURIAC . . .

Morgan wasn't there yet. Further on:

> THE FIRST NUMBER INCLUDED, WITH THE MANIFESTO BY DECOUR AND THE STUDIES BY MAURIAC AND PAULHAN, A POEM BY GEORGES LIMBOUR . . .

Which is when Jacques Decour was arrested and shot. Claude Morgan, named by the Communist Party to replace him, writes further on:

> I HOPED TO BE ABLE TO PRINT NO. 3. PAULHAN GAVE ME SOME ITEMS . . .

Enough. Let Morgan deal with Morgan! Just between us, seeing what it turned into, I'm not very proud of having founded the *Lettres Françaises.* But I'm approaching the heart of this debate.

*
* *

What did I say, precisely? The following: that men on the Left, having for fifty years been most eager to mistreat or reject the homeland, were not, perhaps, without some responsibility for the indifference shown to the homeland by more than one man on the right.

To which Morgan:

> I'M PLEASED TO ANSWER PAULHAN ON THE VERY GROUNDS THAT HE HIMSELF HAS CHOSEN, AND TO SPEAK IN MY TURN ABOUT THE CONCEPT OF THE HOMELAND, WHICH GAINS NOTHING FROM BEING VAGUE.

THIS IDEA, AS WE KNOW ONLY TOO WELL, ALAS!, HAS BEEN CONFUSED BY CERTAIN PEOPLE WITH A NOTION OF CERTAIN ADVANTAGES, THROUGH WHICH THE HOMELAND, SUCH AS IT IS, HAS ENABLED THEM TO PROSPER. LOVE FOR THIS HOMELAND-WHERE-NOTHING-CHANGES, A HIERARCHY OF POWER, CONDITIONS FOR WEALTH, CORPORATE LAW, A LOVE ALWAYS READY TO SPILL THE BLOOD OF OTHERS IN ORDER TO PROTECT ADVANTAGES ACQUIRED, IS ONLY A HORRIBLE LOVE OF SELF. THIS IS THE ONLY THING THE BRASILLACHS, REBATETS AND OTHER DISCIPLES OF MAURRAS COULD IMAGINE. AND WHEN THE WELFARE OF THEIR CLAN COMPELS THEM TO JOIN HANDS WITH THE ENEMY, PATRIOTS LIKE THESE DON'T HESITATE FOR VERY LONG. I TAKE THIS AS A PROVEN FACT.

LOVE OF THE HOMELAND, AMONG DEMOCRATS, IS A LOVE FOR EVERYONE EMBRACED BY THIS HOMELAND, IT'S A LOVE FOR THE NATION (WHICH HAS NOTHING TO DO WITH NATIONALISM), IT'S A LOVE FOR THE PEOPLE, CARE FOR THEIR FREEDOM, THEIR DIGNITY, THEIR HAPPINESS, IT'S AN ACTIVE DESIRE TO RECONNECT THE PEOPLE TO A VALUE-BEARING PAST, GUIDING THEM, ALONG WITH OTHERS, TO A BETTER FUTURE.

AND WHEN IT SEEMS THAT SUCH HAPPINESS CAN BE OBTAINED IN PEACE, THEN THE ONE WHO LOVES HIS HOMELAND IS ABOVE ALL PEACEFUL.

BUT WHEN GERMAN NAZISM AROSE, AND ITS LETHAL DOCTRINE SPREAD ACROSS THE WORLD, THEN EVERYTHING CHANGED, FOR THERE COULD BE NO HAPPINESS IN SLAVERY. AND THE PEOPLE'S HAPPINESS DEMANDED, IN THESE NEW CONDITIONS, THE UPRISING OF A WAR OF LIBERATION AT ANY PRICE AGAINST THE OPPRESSOR. HERE ALL HONEST MEN AGREE. THOSE FOR WHOM THE HOMELAND IS MERELY AN AGGREGATE OF INTERESTS WILL BETRAY IT, WHILE HONEST WRITERS, AND NOT ONLY THOSE OF THE LEFT, BUT FROM LEFT TO RIGHT—AND LET'S FORGET PLATFORMS AND PARTIES, FOR YOU, PAULHAN, WERE AMONG THEM, JUST AS YOU, MAURIAC, WERE AMONG THEM—HAVE ONLY ONE THOUGHT IN COMMON.

THE CONTRADICTION ARGUED SO INGENIOUSLY BY PAULHAN DOESN'T EXIST.

There's more than one minor error here. No, no one could say that the Communist Party sprang to arms in September 1939. But did you follow Claude Morgan's argument? It's more subtle than it first seems. I summarize: the word—and the idea—of *homeland* has two meanings. The fascist uses it to mean his rents, his assets. He sees nothing apart from the carnal homeland, nothing apart from his interests. The democrat, by contrast, thinks first of all about the freedom and dignity of his fellow citizens. Morgan himself has chosen the spiritual homeland. Within every Frenchman is the Human Being he respects and hopes to liberate.

Fine, this is a bit simplistic, but it still derives from a valid observation. When M. Bardèche (who's quite fascist) talks about France, what does he point to? Streets, crops, a French peasant seated at his long table, an old woman waiting in line for milk. He goes so far as to tell us, filling Claude Morgan with satisfaction, that he "loves the race of his country as a breeder loves his flock."[18] But for Julien Benda (who's quite democratic) it's only a question of French truth, of French justice, and—for the French only—of a differentiated brain, capable of separating itself from the national interest. If, in sum, he's nationalist, it's because France is not. Benda loves France because, in his eyes, it lacks a body, a race, ancestors, and crops; Bardèche, because it lacks a soul, honor, and freedom.

The conclusion to be drawn by any normal thinker, it seems to me, is that M. Bardèche and M. Benda should serve, each of them, as a single, solid semipatriot. To obtain the complete Frenchman, it should be enough to combine the two. I don't say that this would be easy, and I don't know that they'd make themselves available. But there's still a problem for all of us: how to become Bardèche and continue to be Benda? How to combine the carnal with the spiritual France in a single love? How to stop being a partisan, and thereby become a patriot?

Claude Morgan, himself, draws an entirely different conclusion: namely, that the contradiction I complained about to those on the left doesn't exist.

His conclusion is very mysterious. What does he mean? Didn't you yourself, Morgan, agree with Marx ten years ago that the proletariat has no homeland, with Thorez that the national defense is strictly a racket, with Aragon that France is the vermin of the world?—I agreed, in effect.—Aren't you saying now that we need to defend France, even at the cost of our lives?—I believe it.—Don't you see a contradiction here?—Not in the least . . .—But isn't it a question of the same France, the same homeland?—That could be.—Then there could be several ways to understand it?—I told you that.—Now I see: the homeland you vomit, wouldn't it be a homeland in the fascist sense?—No doubt.—And the homeland you adore, a homeland in the democratic sense?—Obviously.

For once I follow you, Morgan. But by what right do you pass, without notice, and under the cover of a single word, from one meaning of that word to its opposite? And can't you see that you give the fascist ev-

---

18. *Lettre à François Mauriac,* p. 173.

ery right to do likewise, who, when he says: "Long live the homeland!" understands: "Long live my country and my ancestors and the brave man of street!" But when he says: "Down with the homeland!" he means: "Down with your lethal fantasies, your clouds!"

Ah, finally, stop cheating us, all of you! For, apart from wiles and guiles, there certainly has to be *something* true about the homeland. And I can see only too well how hard it is to ponder that homeland; and how, if we ever hope to find it, we'll have to cut through more than one lie or confusion; and how everything about it is waiting for us—I say: for the best of us—to remake, to reinvent. This is a task worth sharing, at least between men of good will.

M. Maurice Bardèche thinks we could now rebuild, if not the unity of France, then its entente, *if each of us would just admit that he might be wrong. Well (unlikely as it may seem), that's fine with me. Not in 1940, not in 1944, not even in the little notes you've just read, was I ever completely sure of being right.*

But something, I admit, helps me believe somewhat in the virtue of my own cause. It's an indirect or secondary reason (but reasons of this kind may be the best, when direct evidence vanishes in an instant). It's precisely that no one could answer me without resorting to tricks or lies, everyone betraying a common defect, something akin to a central fault: invoking, at every turn, a homeland that no one knows how to believe in.

But do we have to be patriots at all? I can only imagine that the Céné, Benda, Morgan, if truly *patriotic, would argue in a manner more coherent and less lazy. As for dangers . . . I don't deny these: it's only too clear that love for the homeland may eventually prompt us to kill the residents of Munich or Peking (or be killed by them, which is equally vexing). But it still keeps us from slaughtering our brother, our neighbor, our boss—even when they disgust us, even when they hold political views differing from our own. In sum, while a patriot is dangerously vulnerable to national wars, it would be wrong to ignore the fact that he has the good fortune to avoid civil wars.*

NAMES MENTIONED

Andler, Charles (1866–1933): French socialist; professor of German.

Aragon, Louis (1897–1982): writer; Surrealist; prominent Communist party official; friend and foe of Paulhan's for fifty years.

Aulard, Alphonse (1848–1928): writer, historian, and journalist on the Left.

Aveline, Claude (1901–92): writer for the Resistance; author of mystery novels.

Bachelin, Henri (1879–1941): commentator on Rolland.

Bardèche, Maurice (1909–98): right-wing author; brother-in-law of Robert Brasillach.

Beigbeder, Marc (1916–): writer on the Left; biographer of Gide and Sartre.

Benda, Julien (1867–1956): writer and critic on the Left; author, in 1927, of *Les Trahison des Clercs;* a regular contributor to the *Nouvelle Revue Française* (*NRF*).

Benoist, Charles (1861–1936): writer; scholar; member of the Chamber of Deputies; ambassador (1919–24) to the Hague.

Beraud, Henri (1888–1958): right-wing journalist; spent ten years in prison for collaborating.

Berl, Emmanuel (1892–1976): left-wing journalist of pacifist tendencies.

Bernanos, Georges (1888–1948): novelist; lived in Brazil during World War II.

Blanzat, Jean (1906–77): a colleague of Paulhan's on the left; a founder of the Céné (C.N.E.) and the *Lettres Françaises.*

Brasillach, Robert (1909–45): Fascist author and critic; executed as a Nazi collaborator.

Casanova, Laurent (1906–72): Communist party official.

Cassou, Jean (1897–1986): writer, communist; jailed (1941–42) for his Resistance activities.

Céline, Louis-Ferdinand (1896–1961): novelist, pro-German and anti-Semitic; jailed for over a year in Sweden after the war; tried and sentenced in France as a collaborator; pardoned, readmitted to France (1951).

Daladier, Edouard (1884–1970): occasional prime minister of France, 1933–40; committed France against the Germans for the *drôle de guerre.*

Darnand, Joseph (1897–1945): World War I hero; committed fascist and Nazi collaborator; first commander of the Milice, Vichy's paramilitary police force; executed in 1945.

Debû-Bridel, Jacques (1902–93): colleague of Paulhan in the Resistance; a founder of *Editions de Minuit.*

Decour, Jacques (1910–42): communist and colleague of Paulhan in the Resistance; novelist, editor of the *Lettres Françaises* in 1941; executed by the Nazis in 1942.

de Châteaubriant, Alphonse (1877–1951): writer, pro-German and pro-Nazi; director of a collaborationist newspaper.

de Gourmont, Remy (1858–1915): critic, novelist, poet, and anarchist writer.

du Bos, Charles (1882–1939): literary critic for the *Nouvelle Revue Française.*

Drieu la Rochelle, Pierre (1893–1945): fascist, Nazi collaborator; wartime editor of the *Nouvelle Revue Française;* he rescued Paulhan from imprisonment (and possible execution) in 1942; committed suicide in 1945.

Eluard, Paul (1895–1952): poet, communist, and member of the Resistance.

Fabre-Luce, Alfred (1899–1983): right-wing journalist and political writer; jailed after the war.

Ferdonnet, Paul Joseph (1901–45): collaborator; German radio propagandist; known as the *traître de Stuttgart;* executed in 1945.

Giono, Jean (1895–1970): poet and novelist.

Groethuysen, Bernard (1880–1946): German philosopher and sociologist; close friend and colleague of Paulhan.

Guehenno, Jean (1890–1978): left-wing writer and editor.

Guilbeaux, Henri (1896–1980): Marxist editor, novelist, journalist, and pacifist.

Henriot, Emile (1889–1961): journalist.

Jouhandeau, Marcel (1888–1979): writer; fascist sympathizer; friend of Paulhan.

Lagarde, André (1859–1943): historian; disciple of Romain Rolland.

Lamy, Etienne (1846–1919): sociologist.

Larbaud, Valery (1881–1957): poet, author, and reader for the *NRF.*

Laubreaux, Alain (1899–1968): drama critic for the fascist paper *Je Suis Partout.*

Laval, Pierre (1883–1945): leader of the Vichy regime; executed as a collaborator.

Limbour, Georges (1900–1970): literary colleague of Paulhan's.

Marcel, Gabriel (1889–1973): philosopher; member of C.N.E.

Maritain, Jacques (1882–1973): philosopher.

Marsan, Eugène (1882–1936): novelist and monarchist.

Martin-Chauffier, Louis (1894–1980): left-wing writer; member of C.N.E.; regular contributor to pre-World War II *NRF.*

Massis, Henri (1886–1970): journalist.

Mauriac, François (1885–1970): novelist; member of C.N.E.

Maurras, Charles (1868–1952): right-wing author and political leader; founder of Action Française.

Montherlant, Henri de (1896–1972): right-wing author; blacklisted by the C.N.E.

Morgan, Claude (1898–1980): member of the French Communist Party (P.C.F.); editor of the *Lettres Françaises;* member of C.N.E.

Murger, Henri (1822–61): French poet.

Musilier, Emile Henri (1882–1965): French admiral.

Nizan, Paul (1905–40): left-wing writer who broke with the Communist Party in 1939 after the signing of the Stalin-Hitler nonagression pact; killed in action in 1940.

Petitjean, Armand (1913–): Drieu's secretary at the *NRF*; soldier, friend of Paulhan's; author of numerous books.

Poincaré, Raymond (1860–1934): French statesman.

Rebatet, Lucien (1903–72): fascist writer, blacklisted.

Rolland, Romain (1866–1944): famous writer, a pacifist during World War I; author of *Au-dessus de la mêlée* (*Above the Battle*)—a pacifist tract published in 1915.

Salengro, Roger (1890–1936): socialist figure; target of right-wing attacks in late 1930s.

Sazonov, Sergei Dmitryevich (1860–1927): Russian statesman.

Séailles, Gabriel (1852–1922): philosopher.

Therive, André (1891–1967): right-wing critic and novelist.

Thiers, Adolphe (1797–1877): general who crushed the Commune.

Thomas, Edith (1909–70): leftist writer; member of P.C.F.; member of C.N.E.

Thorez, Maurice (1900–1964): head of the P.C.F.; lived in Moscow during World War II.

Vaudal, Jean (1900–1945): leftist colleague of Paulhan's; a cofounder of the *Lettres Françaises.*

Vercors, Jean Bruller (1902–91): founder, with Paulhan, of *Editions de Minuit;* member of C.N.E.

Verhaeren, Emile (1855–1916): Belgian author; opposed to Romain Rolland's pacifism.

Vildrac, Charles (1882–1971): colleague of Paulhan's on the *Lettres Françaises.*

JEAN PAULHAN (1884–1968), a graduate of the Sorbonne and a professional linguist specializing in Malagasy, is the author of numerous works, among them *Le Guerrier appliqué* (1917). He was editor of *Nouvelle Revue Française* from 1925 to 1940, when France was defeated, and again from 1953 until his death.

RICHARD RAND is a professor of English at the University of Alabama. He is the co-translator with John P. Leavey Jr. of Jacques Derrida's *Glas* and the translator of Derrida's *Signsponge*. He has published articles in *Glyph, OLR, Yale French Studies,* and other journals. He is presently at work on a book about lyrical ballads.

The University of Illinois Press
is a founding member of the
Association of American University Presses.

Composed in 10.5/14 Adobe Minion
with Adobe Minion display
by Jim Proefrock
at the University of Illinois Press
Designed by Dennis Roberts
Manufactured by Maple-Vail
Book Manufacturing Group

University of Illinois Press
1325 South Oak Street
Champaign, IL 61820-6903
www.press.uillinois.edu